No
HIGHWAY
CODE

Ivor Baddiel & Jonny Zucker

First published in Great Britain in 2006
by Weidenfeld & Nicolson
10 9 8 7 6 5 4 3 2 1

A CIP catalogue record for this book
is available from the British Library.

ISBN-13: 978 0 304 36812 9
ISBN-10: 0 304 36812 1

Designed by Nova White (www.novawhite.co.uk)
Illustrations by Ruth Murray (www.ruthmurray.net)

Printed in Italy

The Orion Publishing Group's policy is to use papers that
are natural, renewable and recyclable products and made
from wood grown in sustainable forests. The logging and
manufacturing processes are expected to conform to the
environmental regulations of the country of origin.

Weidenfeld & Nicolson
The Orion Publishing Group Ltd
Orion House
5 Upper Saint Martin's Lane
London WC2H 9EA
www.orionbooks.co.uk

Not THE HIGHWAY CODE

Ivor Baddiel & Jonny Zucker

The Unofficial Rules of the Road

WEIDENFELD & NICOLSON

To all the traffic wardens, boy racers, Sunday drivers, tractors, herds of cattle, roadworks, HGV drivers, learner drivers, rollerbladers, clampers, little old lady drivers, horses, road ragers, white van drivers, taxi drivers and town planners, without whom this book would not have been possible.

Contents

INTRODUCTION

The so-called 'real' *Highway Code* purports to contain all the rules of the road. To this we say, quite categorically, BOLLOCKS. Where is the rule that states if traffic lights turn amber as you approach them, put your foot down and drive like MICHAEL SCHUMACHER to get through? Where is the rule that states you'll always fasten your seat belt thirty seconds into your journey – nearly causing a FATAL accident? Where is the rule that states diversions never, ever lead you back to where you want to be?

We'll tell you exactly where those rules are; they're in here, *Not the Highway Code*. This is the REAL ROAD-USERS BIBLE, the one you should be studying before you're allowed to drive.

Of course, it won't help you pass your driving test, but then, passing your driving test won't help you drive either. This work is hewn out of years of experience; years of sitting in AGONISINGLY SLOW-MOVING TRAFFIC; years of tolerating the lurid clothing worn by cyclists; years of spending years trying to find a parking space. Because that's what's really going on out there. (That and lots more.)

So if you want to SURVIVE on the streets, put your (metaphorical) ignition key into this book and take it for a (metaphorical) spin. If it makes just one person a better, more responsible driver, we'll be astonished.

Wanker

1.RULES FOR PEDESTRIANS

General guidance

Use your feet – this is the minimum entry requirement for anyone wishing to use the title 'pedestrian'.

Never make eye contact with other pedestrians – there are a number of reasons for this:

• they might be hard and beat you up

• you might end up having to talk to someone who you really don't want to and whose name you can't for the life of you remember

• you might owe them money

• they might ask you for money

• they might fall instantly in love with you and stalk you for the rest of your life.

If someone is walking directly towards you, never give ground, always let them move out of the way – if you do move one way to allow them to pass, they will also move that way and you will end up stuck in a seemingly endless pavement dance that will eventually form the central plank of a new REALITY TV SHOW. The longest recorded such dance occurred in Melbourne, Australia, when two pedestrians, each heavily laden down with bags of shopping, moved the same way in unison for four years, seven months, thirteen days, five hours, twenty-eight minutes and six seconds. The deadlock was only broken when one of them DIED.

Pedestrians should always be on the lookout for uneven pavements and walking hazards. On seeing such a hazard, head directly towards it and ensure you trip on one of the upturned slabs. The resulting injury will allow you to sue the local authority for millions and should ensure a considerable amount of time off work. (Note: You can also SUE THE LOCAL COUNCIL FOR MILLIONS if you trip over a feather while walking along the pavement, even if the feather fell out of a RED INDIAN HEADDRESS that you were wearing because you were on your way to a fancy dress party.)

If the temperature goes above 15° Celsius, all young male pedestrians whose bodies are toned through years of drinking lager and scoffing fast food, must instantly take their tops off and walk around bare-chested.

If you're a female pedestrian and you suffer the humiliation of a wolf whistle while walking past a BUILDING SITE, enter the building site, having of course first put on a hard hat, find the offending wolf whistler and prove that you are not just a SEX OBJECT by engaging him in a lengthy discussion about Minimalist Architecture in post-war Cuba. That should ensure that he thinks twice before WOLF WHISTLING the next time a fantastic bird walks past the site.

If you're a male pedestrian walking past a building site and someone wolf whistles at you, take the whistler to the European Court of Human Rights – it's in Brussels and there are plenty of nice, cheap hotels. Get a room and spend a romantic weekend together.

If someone in a car winds down the window and asks you for directions, be under no illusion, they will not listen to a single word you say. Therefore, for your own amusement, why not recite the LORD'S PRAYER or perhaps the entire lyrics of Les Misérables?

Crossing the road

As a pedestrian cars are your natural enemy. You have your territory and they have theirs and it is best if it stays that way, but if you absolutely have to cross a road, the following guidelines should be observed as closely as possible.

Zebra crossings – as a British pedestrian, these are great places to cross the road. No matter how fast a car is going in the UK it will stop to let even the most bag-laden OLD LADY cross on a zebra crossing. Furthermore, the car will remain stationary until all pedestrians have fully crossed the road, regardless of how long they take, so, when crossing, take your time. Amble, stroll or, if you fancy, LAY DOWN A RUG AND HAVE A PICNIC. Be advised though; elsewhere in the world this does not apply and if you step out onto a zebra crossing in a foreign nation expecting cars to stop, you will most probably be MOWN DOWN.

**Pedestrians taking a well deserved
break from crossing the road**

Traffic light crossings – not as good as zebra
crossings as the time you have to cross the road
is limited, but there is fun to be had in annoying
cars by pressing the button and then not
crossing the road.

AQUARIAN CAR (bought between 20 Jan – 19 Feb)
Romance is in the air. Treat yourself to a wash 'n wax
and go get 'em hot rod.

The green man:

If you see a green man flashing,
alert the police immediately.

If you see a green woman flashing, flash her
back; if she doesn't run away, you're in.

The Green Cross Code – this is a code that
helps teach children to cross a road safely,
though apparently it also works for adults.

• **Find a safe place to cross** – this can take
anywhere from ten seconds to three weeks.

• **Stop just before you get to the kerb** –
this refers to the kerb you are crossing from.
If you stop before you get to the kerb you are
crossing to you will be stopping in the middle
of the road and might DIE.

• **Look all around for traffic and listen** –
this is crucial. Looking just left and right will not
suffice. You must look up, down, behind you,
diagonally behind you to the left, diagonally
behind you to the right and into the FOURTH
DIMENSION just to be sure. People that fail to
cover all their bases have been hit by gliders,
25th-century burrowing craft and time machines
returning from both the future and the past.

• **When it is SAFE, go straight across the road**
– do not run. This is true for all people other
than those who are intending to COMMIT
SUICIDE, in which case the rule is, when it
is UNSAFE, go straight across the road.

Lollipop ladies – using one of these ladies (and sometimes gentlemen) is one of the easiest and safest ways to get across a road. Essentially they take all the hardship out of reaching the opposite pavement by flinging themselves into the middle of the road and forcing all oncoming traffic to stop instantly. (HITTING AND INJURING a lollipop lady (and sometimes gentleman) is punishable by DEATH, so the traffic does generally stop.) The pedestrian can then cross safely and at his or her leisure.

To become a lollipop lady (and sometimes gentleman) you have to be retired, extremely lonely and not averse to wearing a yellow jacket that, along with the Great Wall of China, can be seen from the Moon.

**A lollipop lady (or possibly gentleman)
as seen from the moon**

Pedestrians in the country

There is often no pavement or footpath on country roads due to natural erosion and CRAP LOCAL COUNCILS, but, if you do find yourself walking along such a road, take extra care. It is illegal not to be DRUNK while driving in the country and hence, even on roads where there are pavements you're likely to be knocked down. Where there are no pavements, you might as well have the LAST RITES read to you before you set out.

Eye contact – if you do make eye contact with someone while being a pedestrian in the country, in an attempt to prove how much more friendly they are than people in towns, they will be just that, friendly. However, their idea of friendliness involves making polite conversation about the weather, MUCK SPREADING, exchanging tedious country proverbs and discussing next year's harvest, all topics that would bore the PANTS off someone wearing extremely tight-fitting PANTS that have been superglued on.

Ramblers – pedestrians in the country are called ramblers. These people are fanatical about walking and will walk through your living room, your bedroom and your TOILET citing the 'right to roam' as justification for doing so. If you live in the country and a group of ramblers do appear in your house, remain calm and simply tell them that the people next door won't allow ramblers to walk through their kitchen. This will result in said ramblers stomping over there and organising a demonstration and leaflet campaign, before you can shout:

'GET OFF MY LAND YOU FILTHY PEASANTS!'

Ramblers exercising their right to roam

2. RULES ABOUT ANIMALS

Horses

Riding a horse on a public highway – make sure that when you ride past a car, you do so really slowly and quietly as any sudden movement or noise may cause the car to bolt.

Horse excrement – unlike dog owners, if your horse relieves itself while out on the road, you do not have to place the excrement in a bag and dispose of it. What you have to do is leave it exactly where it is so that as many people as possible step in it – this is especially true of police horses at football matches.

Horseboxes – if your horse breaks down you have to transport it to the vet in a horsebox. If the vet declares your horse a write-off, you have to transport it to France so that it can be eaten or TURNED INTO GLUE.

Dogs

Guide dogs for the blind – intelligent as these animals are, under no circumstances should they be allowed to drive for blind people.

In cars – the correct way to position a dog in a vehicle is to open the window just enough for the dog to stick its head out, then stick the dog's head out and set off.

Nodding dogs – these are off-putting to other drivers, cheap and not particularly funny. They just about make the cut for Christmas stocking fillers.

**Don't let Rover
drive the Rover**

Insects

Bees and wasps – if a bee or wasp flies into the
car while you are driving the only thing you can
do is panic. Flay your arms wildly about your
head, shout, SCREAM AND LOSE CONTROL
of your feet to such an extent that you floor
the accelerator and go hurtling into the car in
front. Don't worry if the end result is a 15-CAR
PILE-UP with MULTIPLE FATALITIES; whatever
happens, it'll be better than being stung.

Other animals

Herds – it is not uncommon when driving along
country lanes to find oneself stuck behind a herd
of animals. There is nothing you can do but sit in
your car and wait until the road is clear.
However, to make you feel better, at a later date
you might like to take your car into their field and
drive around really slowly in front of any animals
that are moving about.

Chickens – although fabled in the classic joke, the reality is that chickens rarely cross roads; hence, one might well argue that the question one should really ask is why didn't the chicken cross the road? To which, of course, the answer is because he'd left his waistcoat at home.

Hedgehogs – hedgehogs on the other hand have a remarkable propensity to cross roads. Or more accurately, attempt to cross roads. They do this because in hedgehog lore it is written (and so it shall be) that the first hedgehog to successfully cross a road will be anointed as the hedgehog MESSIAH and lead all hedgehogs back to the Promised Land, an allotment just OUTSIDE DUNSTABLE. So far none have been successful. In fact so many have been flattened that some councils have let the number of flattened hedgehogs on the road build up to a certain height so that they can then cover them with concrete – the resulting mound makes a perfectly good road hump, saving the council, and you, the council-tax payer, a lot of MONEY.

General

Eating animals while driving – it is permissible to consume hamburgers, kebabs, fish and the like while in control of your vehicle. However, they must be cooked prior to setting off on your journey and not once on the road, even if you have the facility to plug a LEAN MEAN GRILLING MACHINE into your cigarette lighter.

3. RULES FOR CYCLISTS

The rules in this section are for all road users who choose to make their journey by unicycle, bicycle (with or without stabilisers), tandem, tricycle or penny-farthing. The basic rule is that you do not have to follow any other rules of the highway and must cause as much ANNOYANCE and IRRITATION to other roads users as possible.

Clothing – you should wear:

A cycle helmet. It will make you look like a complete idiot but years of scientific research have failed to unravel the great mystery as to why it is impossible to design a bike helmet that does not make you look like a COMPLETE KNOBHEAD. So, until the boffins unravel that one, you're lumbered.

IMPORTANT: Don't be fooled into thinking that the SLIGHTLY POINTIER helmets that professional cyclists wear will make you look cool. They won't.

Latex shorts that are so tight they cut off the BLOOD SUPPLY below your knees, ironically making it difficult to cycle.

A combination of colours that would make Jonathan Ross RETCH, or wetch, as he would say. It's part of the Be Safe, Be Seen philosophy, but in truth the philosophy is more Be Safe, Be Seen, HAVE NO SOCIAL LIFE.

At night:

Is the best time to go cycling, as fewer people will see you and thus know you're a cyclist.

When cycling:

Never, ever stop at red lights. This is paramount. In the cycling world, red, amber and green all mean go – go as fast as you can, LAUGHING MANIACALLY at the car drivers gridlocked behind you.

Never, ever stop at zebra crossings. These are akin to the chequered flags at the end of Formula 1 races and therefore cyclists must zoom across them as fast as possible, paying SCANT REGARD to pedestrians crossing the road.

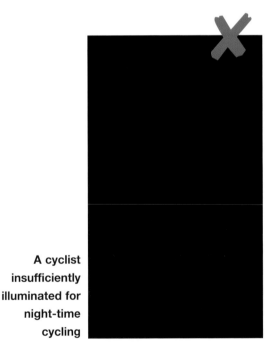

A cyclist insufficiently illuminated for night-time cycling

Never, ever put your feet on the ground. On the rare occasion that you are forced to stop by some INCONSIDERATE car driver, bounce up and down on your bike as if CAVORTING ON A POGO STICK. If your feet do touch the ground you will be forever ex-communicated from the cycling community.

Never, ever travel in a straight line; always weave in and out of traffic. Unlike cars, which have to drive on the left, the entire road space is your domain; you can cycle on the left, right, up on the pavement, over cars or wherever you choose.

The rule when cycling at night is simple:
BE SAFE, BE SEEN, BLIND OTHERS.

Signalling:

As a general rule there is no need to signal. Other road users should MIND THEIR OWN BUSINESS; they do not need to know your intentions.

If, however, you would like to use signals, the following are particularly useful.

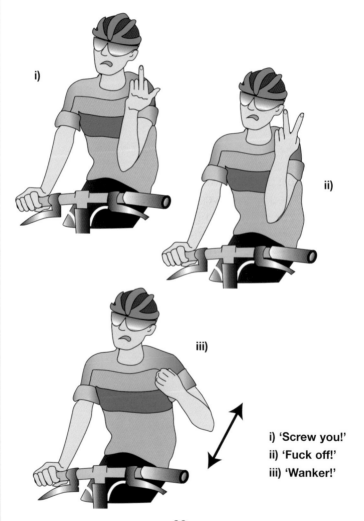

i)

ii)

iii)

i) 'Screw you!'
ii) 'Fuck off!'
iii) 'Wanker!'

4. RULES FOR MOTORCYCLISTS

The following rules are absolutely essential for all motorcyclists, there are no exceptions whatsoever under any circumstances, unless you're a HELL'S ANGEL, in which case please feel free to break any of these rules, your majesty (and don't hurt me).

General

On all journeys, the rider and pillion passenger must wear protective helmets. However, once a crash helmet has been involved in a crash or dropped on the floor, you should replace it and sell the old one on EBAY.

You should also consider wearing strong, suitable clothing – leathers are generally preferred, though vegetarians can now buy leather substitutes made out of TOFU – these look and smell just like leathers and make a tasty snack on long journeys. (OK, they make an untasty snack on long journeys.)

You must not carry more than one pillion passenger unless you're part of a motorcycle display team, in which case you're allowed to carry up to thirty-four passengers, but only in a pyramid formation.

Scooters and mopeds are not motorbikes, their only functions are

• to deliver pizza.

• to provide transport for trainee London taxi drivers learning 'the knowledge.

• to take part in Mod versus Rockers battle re-enactments on piers in South England on bank holidays.

In any large conurbation, the likelihood is that your bike will be stolen. To ensure this doesn't happen make sure you DON'T OWN ONE.

Middle-aged men – middle-aged men will often buy and ride around on very big bikes. In fact, the bike manufacturers have cottoned on to this and you can now buy a Honda Mid-Life Crisis, a YAMAHA VIAGRA and a Suzuki I'm Leaving You For Someone Younger. Try not to laugh openly at them as if they see you their WHOLE SENSE OF SELF WORTH WILL CRUMBLE and they may well have an accident.

PISCES CAR (bought between 20 Feb – 20 March)
Whatever you do don't go out today. You will crash.

Daylight riding

- Make yourself visible.

Driving in the dark

- Make yourself more visible.

Manoeuvring

As a vehicle with a great capacity to accelerate the temptation to burn up cars and weave in and out of them whilst CACKLING HYSTERICALLY can be overwhelming. But be warned, car drivers are canny customers and it has been known for some time now that they invented the **'blind spot'** purely to allow them to say, ' I didn't see him/her when I pulled out suddenly and sent them FLYING TO KINGDOM COME.'

INTERESTING FACT

(Pedestrians) Sophia Svetoshtinka, a Bulgarian peasant, has been named Pedestrian of the Year on no less than 15 separate occasions.

5. RULES FOR DRIVERS AND MOTORCYCLISTS

Vehicle Condition

Your vehicle must have the following:

- an engine
- brakes
- wheels including steering wheel
- doors
- roof
- novelty air freshener
- circular tin of hard-boiled travel sweets
- a leather-bound copy of the *Magna Carta*

There are three types of vehicle condition:

Brand New – this only ever exists in a car showroom.

Banger – the condition your car is in the moment it leaves the car showroom, when its value decreases by 89.6 PER CENT.

Old Banger – the condition your car is in twenty minutes after leaving the car showroom, when its value will have decreased by 97.08 PER CENT.

In any of these conditions you must ensure that your car is roadworthy, which means it has to be worthy of the roads it is to be driven on. By taking a quick glance at the majority of roads, you'll realise that RAMSHACKLE, FALLING APART, A DISGRACE, UNFIT and DANGEROUS are all roadworthy states.

ently on the road are milk-floats.'

If your car has a scratch down one side it is imperative that you have one of exactly the same dimensions, in exactly the same place on the other side. Nobody likes an asymmetrical car.

If your car or van is particularly dusty, someone will always come along and write 'CLEAN ME' or 'ALSO COMES IN WHITE' in the dust (in exceptional circumstances people will write an abridged version of Chaucer's *The Miller's Tale*). Ironically, the way to avoid this is to take the first piece of advice and actually CLEAN THE CAR.

Before setting off

Before you start any SHORT JOURNEY you should ensure that you have a destination in mind and are not going to spend hours driving around aimlessly, unless it is a Sunday and you are participating in the activity known as 'TAKING THE FAMILY FOR A DRIVE' a pastime unique to Great Britain, which involves a directionless journey lasting precisely one hour and seventeen minutes.

Before you start any LONG JOURNEY you should ensure:

• **You've been to the toilet 18 times** – particularly true of children and PREGNANT WOMEN.

• **You don't forget anything.** Be especially careful not to forget your 'DON'T FORGET' checklist.

You've checked all weather reports (newspaper, radio, TV, internet, phone lines, DRUID PREDICTIONS). This will avoid unnecessary impediments to your journey, such as putting crampons on your tyres on a scolding hot day.

You can shut the boot – especially essential when transporting dead bodies/large stashes of illegal goods. If you can't shut the boot, then question whether all of the items you have packed are essential. For example, is that third DIDGERIDOO really necessary? Can you get by without a life-sized cardboard cut out of Wayne Rooney? Would GRANDMA be more comfortable on the roof rack?

Vehicle towing and loading

Paris Hilton going away for the weekend

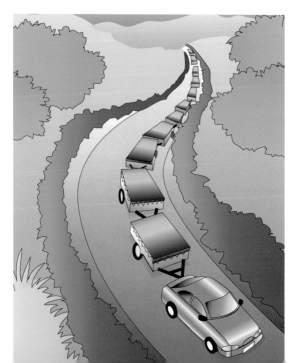

You **MUST NOT** overload a trailer if you have one. If the one you're loading does reach its limit, simply add another trailer onto the first one and load that one until it becomes full, when you can add another one. This process can continue until the nationally agreed limit of eighteen trailers has been reached.

IT IS ILLEGAL to tow a tow truck. It's illegal to tow a tow truck towing a tow truck. However, IT IS LEGAL to tow a truck with a tow truck towing a truck with a tow truck in it.

If you're sitting in a car being towed by another car, don't get annoyed at not being able to overtake the car towing you. Also, whatever you do, don't slam on the brakes or try to carry out a three-point turn.

Seat belts

The law in this country states that you have to wear seat belts in a moving car. This means that if you are in a stop-start TRAFFIC JAM, it is permissible to unbuckle the belt when stationary, as long as you buckle up again as soon as you start moving.

At one time, in order to remind people to wear seat belts, the GOVERNMENT ran an advertising campaign telling drivers to 'Clunk-Click' every trip. However, modern-day seat belts don't make that sound, so you are now advised to download your particular seat-belt sound from ITUNES or Napster onto your car stereo, as an aide-memoire for seat-belt use.

For some reason it is impossible to remember to buckle up before you actually set off on your journey. You generally remember somewhere between five and thirty seconds after you leave. This means you then have to concentrate on the road while simultaneously trying to pull the seat belt over you and 'click' it in place. This has proved so difficult that the RAC are now offering a part-time course in BASIC CONTORTIONISM.

Children in cars

Children hate journeys. They get bored, irritable and angry, and start speaking in special, whiny voices. The world record for asking 'ARE WE THERE YET?' is held by Bridget Sykes from Crewe, who managed to ask the question 11,000 times between her hometown and Nuneaton.

There are a million ways to occupy children on car journeys. If you don't have the money to buy those flashy back-of-seat DVD players, then you may wish to use traditional travel games such as 'I SPY', 'I don't spy', 'I thought I spied' and 'I undercover government agent'.

For any children under fourteen who are reading this, it is imperative to understand the following: When your mum or dad says 'we're nearly there now' they are lying. To avoid such untruths it is worth carrying your own map and compass.

Other lies parents tell children in cars include:

'No honestly, I don't mind that you've just THROWN UP over my new leather seat covers.'

'No, it's quite OK for you to repeatedly kick the back of my seat even though I have a serious SPINAL INJURY.'

With younger children you'll need to allow plenty of time to gather together all the accoutrements you need – the basic rule is three hours per child.

Whatever you do don't forget your child's 'Special Thing'. This can be a doll, a bear or a tattered dribble-stained piece of cloth known as a 'raggy'. If you do forget it, your child will, SCREAM, KICK, PUNCH, BITE, TEAR THEIR HAIR OUT, POO or WEE the entire journey. (Exception can be made if your child's 'Special Thing' is a decomposing lizard.)

Fitness to drive

Don't drive if you are tired. If your eyelids keep drooping, your head lolls forward and you keeping imagining yourself wearing your favourite pyjamas and sipping a MUG OF COCOA, you are dangerously tired and are doing what is termed 'falling asleep at the wheel'. If this happens ask any passengers who may be in the car with you to slap you repeatedly around the face so that you stay awake. If no passengers are in the car you may SELF-FLAGELLATE using jump leads.

If you do feel weary:

STOP at an extremely expensive service station. You may have to take out a BRIDGING LOAN to pay for a cup of outrageously weak and tasteless coffee, but you'll be so FUMING at the price that you won't be able to relax enough to sleep at the wheel.

Getting fit for driving involves building up just one muscle group – your ankle muscles (probably called your ankotarsals or something like that, but this isn't a physiology book and we can't be bothered to look it up). The best way to do this is to drive a lot.

Vision – you must be able to read a vehicle number plate from a distance of 20.5 metres, about five car-lengths. This must be achieved without any of the following visual aids: a magnifying glass; a friend standing right in front of the car and shouting out the number plate; the HUBBLE TELESCOPE.

Alcohol and Drugs

Drink driving is not a good idea, primarily because you'll spill most of your pint while manoeuvring.

Pissed drivers – try and avoid these as much as possible, especially if they are members of the ROYAL FAMILY; no matter how PISSED they are, they will not be the ones who lose their licence and have to do 200 HOURS COMMUNITY SERVICE.

Stoned drivers – on the whole these are utterly harmless. For the most part they will be doing 10 mph when the speed limit is 50 mph and stopping at every green light, including those in the front of SHOP DISPLAYS at SPAR STORES. To be honest, the stoned driver may only be driving in his or her head and not actually in a car on the road. In these instances, the chances of an accident are minimal.

6. GENERAL RULES, TECHNIQUES AND ADVICE FOR ALL DRIVERS AND RIDERS

This section should be read by all road users, though preferably not while actually using the road.

Signals

The horn – a horn must only be used in exceptional circumstances as follows:

• when passing a striking or protesting group in order to show SOLIDARITY.

• if your football team wins a trophy

• if you see someone you know in the street and want them to see you so you can wave at them.

• if the car in front remains motionless for longer than 1.8 seconds for no obvious reason.

• if the car two in front remains motionless for longer than 2.6 seconds and the car directly in front hasn't honked

• to show displeasure at the car behind honking you for remaining motionless for longer than 1.8 seconds for no obvious reason

• to test it and make sure it's working properly

• to let someone you're picking up know you have arrived at their house to pick them up thus saving you the terrible hassle of having to get out of the car to ring their doorbell

• if an attractive woman is seen
      (for male and lesbian drivers only)

• if an attractive man is seen
      (for women and gay male drivers only)

• if an attractive man or woman is seen
      (for bisexual men and women only)

• if someone cuts you up

• if someone is driving really slowly in front of you, such as a learner driver

• and so on for another 4,923 REASONS.

Probably not a police officer >>>

Police stopping procedures:

Siren – if the police put their siren on and don't fly past you at the speed of light, it is you they want to talk to. If you have a CORPSE in the boot of your car or cash in the REGION of £50,000 and above, put your foot down and get away from them as quickly as possible. Alternatively, if you are completely innocent but fancy appearing on 'The World's Wildest, Wackiest and Weirdest Police Chases' then do likewise.

Directing you to pull over – if a police officer is standing in the middle of the road and directing you to pull over, do not panic. They are probably carrying out routine inspections. If a SEMI-NAKED man covered in blood is gesturing for you to do likewise, do panic. He is probably a SERIAL KILLER carrying out a ROUTINE KILLING.

Lighting requirements

You **MUST** use headlights:

- at night even if you're blind
- when proving to someone that your headlights work
- during the day if there's a total eclipse of the sun

You **MUST NOT** use headlights:

If they are the type of headlights that come up from underneath the bonnet. There is no clearer indication that the driver is a TWAT. If you value your social standing one jot you'll have them removed and replaced with NON-TWATTY ordinary headlights.

To dazzle anyone – if unsure as to how bright your lights can be before they dazzle someone, watch Close Encounters of the Third Kind, particularly that bit where the spaceship lands and there's lots of light. That level is too bright.

Hazard warning lights – the great myth about hazard warning lights is that once you turn them on YOU CAN PARK ANYWHERE: yellow lines, double yellow lines, red lines, zigzags, loading bays and traffic wardens' heads. Sadly, the powers-that-be have become wise to this little trick and will rub salt in the wound by pulling up alongside in the clamping vehicle and putting its hazards on whilst clamping you.

CONTROL OF THE VEHICLE

Braking

Use brakes

• to test if SOMEONE is up your ARSE too much – the way to test this is to slam your brakes on suddenly; if the person behind crashes into you, they were up your arse too much.

• to test if YOU'RE up someone's ARSE too much – the way to test this is to slam your brakes on and wait five seconds. If the car in front is still less than 5 feet away, you were up their arse too much.

• if you're worried you're going to crash – the way to test this is to slam your brakes on and shut your eyes tightly; if you don't hear a crunching sound followed by a shattering-of-glass sound followed by an 'OH MY GOD I'M DYING' sound, you've probably just about got away with it.

• during your driving test when the instructor slams a book or hand down on the dashboard.

Do not use brakes

• when RAM RAIDING
• when JOY RIDING
• if you like CRASHING into things
• when trying to break the LAND SPEED RECORD

Annoying braking – certain drivers will brake every three seconds whether they need to or not. These 'brake addicts' or 'braddicts' are seriously ill people. An extended period of therapy is one option, though the preferred treatment is to disable the car's brakes, rendering them inoperative, and then send the driver out to one of those roads in Australia that is straight for something like 3,000 miles.

Speed limits

Exceeding the limit – in days of yore if you exceeded the speed limit a police officer would pull you over and say, 'All right Stirling Moss, how fast do we think we were going then?' (Police officers often use the third person because on the whole they are very lonely, UNHAPPY INDIVIDUALS and by doing so they get some sense of having 'friends'.) You would then say, 'Er, 29 officer, sir.' To which the constable would reply, 'Oh yeah, and I'm the QUEEN MUM.' Nowadays this witty and jovial exchange is all but extinct thanks to speed cameras, which will at best mutter, 'YEAH, WHATEVER' when you attempt to enter into a dialogue with them.

Autobahn – there is no speed limit on Germany's autobahn, consequently traffic cops assigned there have been known to DIE OF BOREDOM.

Stopping distances

In theory a two-second gap between you and the car in front should give ample time to stop. In practice, whoever thought that up has clearly never experienced rush hour in a major city when you're lucky if you have a 0.00001-second gap to stop in – though to be fair, you're not going to be going very fast anyway.

In the country it is best to leave a nine-hour gap, as that is the length of time you're going to be stuck behind a tractor.

If you can read this you're too close – if a car has this sign on its back bumper, you don't want to stop – you want to smash straight into the back of the car to teach the driver a lesson for being such a TOSSER. Your excuse is that you were too distracted reading the BUMPER STICKER.

INTERESTING FACT

(Learner Drivers) In Paraguay it is permissible to kill learner drivers if they fail to get out of your way quickly enough.

MULTI-LANE CARRIAGEWAYS

Changing lanes – as everyone knows the correct procedure when changing lanes is mirror, signal, manoeuvre: look in the mirror, if all's clear, bung on the indicator and move out. However, the degree to which someone is a crap driver can be worked out by how much they diminish this rule. Dropping the mirror bit and just doing signal, manoeuvre makes them A BIT CRAP. Dropping the mirror and signal bit and just manoeuvring makes them really crap. And getting them in completely the wrong order such that they end up doing manoeuvre, signal, mirror makes them OFF THEIR TITS ON LSD or a foreign diplomat.

On a three-lane carriageway

• use the left-hand lane if you're a pensioner, a vicar or a BOY RACER overtaking someone on the inside.

• use the middle lane if you're a middle-lane hogger, if you're undertaking to overtake an undertaker or if you're undertaking someone overtaking someone in the right hand lane

• use the right-hand lane to overtake someone in the middle lane and someone in the left-hand lane, overtake someone in the middle lane overtaking someone in the left-hand lane and OVERTAKE AN UNDERTAKER in the middle lane undertaking to overtake someone in the left-hand lane.

You, as seen through the eyes of an irate cyclist »»

Two-lane hogger – certain drivers can never decide which lane they want to drive in. They STRADDLE the line between two lanes boldly declaring, 'Look at me, I have a wheel in both camps!' In reality they have nothing to be proud of. Their indecision on the road is a manifestation of their indecision in life. They are weak-willed, LILY-LIVERED types only fit for the most junior jobs in the most mundane professions.

Cycle lanes – even though cyclists don't have to obey any of the rules that apply to other road users, when it comes to their sacrosanct little areas, transgress and you're in big trouble. If you so much as accidentally let a wheel of your car scrape the edge of a cycle lane, an irate cyclist will appear out of nowhere and harangue you MERCILESSLY, weaving around your car declaring that you're no better than SATAN HIMSELF.

Bus lanes – bus lanes are the non-motorway equivalent of hard shoulders; miles and miles of open road that you long to use so that you can get out of the traffic jam you're currently in. Whatever you do though, don't give in to temptation or you'll receive a HEFTY FINE. The only thing you can do is become a bus driver – though you'll then be restricted to the route and unless everywhere you ever want to go to is actually on that route, you're in trouble. Alternatively, you could BUY A BUS and drive around in that; even though that defeats the whole point of bus lanes – to transport a large number of people quickly and efficiently – prosecuting you for driving your own bus in a bus lane is legally PREPOSTEROUS.

Driving on one-way streets – the crucial thing about one-way streets is to make yourself fully cognisant as to which way that one-way is. The right way is the way you want, not the wrong way.

GENERAL ADVICE

24. You must not

• drive the way you were taught by your driving instructor.

• drive with any consideration for other road users.

• WASH YOUR CAR on any day other than a SUNDAY.

Adapt your driving where necessary.
In particular:

• Don't observe the local speed limit while participating in a FORMULA 1 race.

• Take the road condition into account. Where there are a lot of potholes be sure to drive over them in the hope of causing yourself a nasty, though not fatal injury. Depending on the extent of the injury you'll then be able to SUE THE LOCAL COUNCIL FOR MILLIONS and possibly never have to work again.

• If the driver of the car that has just cut you up is elderly honk your horn and flick them a 'V' SIGN. If they have a SPIDERS WEB TATTOO covering their face give them your wallet.

Safe driving needs concentration. Avoid distractions when driving such as

> **doing** a 10,000 piece jigsaw
> **counselling** married couples
> **rehearsing** a scene from *Hamlet*
> **thinking**
> **trainspotting**

Mobile phones and in-car technology

You must not use a hand-held mobile phone when driving a car but there is no law that says you can't use an ordinary landline phone in a car, though you'll need varying miles of phone wire, depending on where you're going.

Only use your mobile phone to make really important calls like ringing home to say you'll be back in ten minutes, and then ringing again in five minutes to say you'll be back in eight minutes (you always underestimate the traffic).

Satellite navigation systems

The voice – the voices used for satellite navigation systems are always incredibly ANNOYING, PATRONISING and SLIGHTLY CREEPY – 'In 200 metres, turn left.' You can hear it can't you? Also, it may be an illusion, but if you don't follow the route it is telling you to it seems to become ever so slightly IRRITATED, which in turn irritates you. The best thing you can do is record yourself saying, 'No, I'm not going to turn left, what are you going to do about it?' and play it in response.

The route – satellite navigation systems will always take you via the longest, most congested route doing the exact opposite of what is promised on the back of the expansive and EXPENSIVE PACKAGING.

In slow-moving traffic

Let one car out of a side road, but never two – sometimes a second car will try and sneak in; if they do, drive as quickly as you can to reduce the gap, thus preventing them getting in.

When the car in front of you moves, wait a little while until there is a fair distance between your two cars, then you'll be able to make up the gap by driving fairly quickly, thus creating the illusion that you are not stuck in slow-moving traffic.

The general pattern when in slow-moving traffic is as follows:

• **first ten minutes – you'll be relatively** CALM, though aware of the beginnings of stress building up.

• **second ten minutes – you'll be tapping you fingers in an annoyed fashion on the steering wheel and getting** QUITE ANGRY.

• **third ten minutes – you will have long-since fallen out with your fellow passengers, be** BANGING YOUR HEAD on the steering wheel repeatedly and soon be screaming OBSCENITIES at anyone and anything.

• **fourth ten minutes – you'll take the train.**

Driving in built-up areas

Narrow residential streets – if you're a teenage boy on a scooter drive as fast as you can, predominantly at midnight.

Traffic calming measures

Road humps – there is currently a road hump
PANDEMIC sweeping the nation. If left
uncurtailed the entire country will resemble
a cobbled street, but without any of its olde
worldy, MEWSY CHARM.

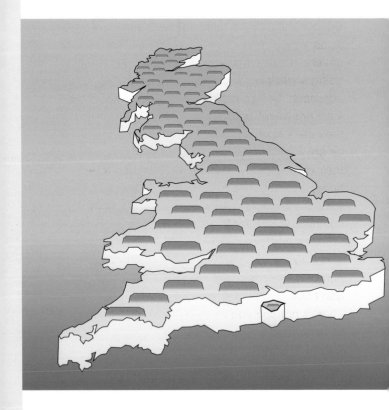

**How the UK will look in 2009 if the road hump
pandemic is uncurtailed**

e there and it's pretty grim.'

> ## INTERESTING FACT
> (Cyclists) The largest saddle sore was recorded in 1986. It covered the entire left arse cheek of Belgian Bastia Plumagereux and was encroaching on the right cheek. To stem its progress doctors had to amputate his buttocks.

Speed at which to tackle road humps – this is, as yet, a SCIENTIFIC UNKNOWN. Some drivers, especially taxi drivers, prefer the 'I'm going so slowly I'm practically stationary' approach. Others prefer the 'I'm going to act as if it's not there' approach. Others still will retain their car's speed, but approach the hump at an angle and then there are those who floor their car until they get to the very edge of the hump and then break heavily – in EXTREME CIRCUMSTANCES this can result in the car somersaulting over the hump in question.

The road hump you forget about – in any humped road there will always be one hump you don't see and thus drive over as if it's not there. There's nothing you can do about this, it's akin to forgetting your MOTHER-IN-LAW'S BIRTHDAY or your wedding anniversary, so just live with it.

> ARIES CAR (bought between 21 March – 20 April)
> Your rear tyres are not getting on. Change the left one for the spare, it's far more easy going and laid back.

7. USING THE ROAD

GENERAL RULES

Before moving off you should make sure that:

• you have a vehicle near you

• you are inside this vehicle.

Once moving you should:

Keep to the left side of the road. Amongst those who have recently returned from holidays abroad, there is a tendency to drive on the right as they are still in 'vacation mode.' This is UNNECESSARY, PRETENTIOUS and DANGEROUS.

Keep both of your hands on the wheel unless the person in the passenger seat has just handed you a cup of HOT SCALDING COFFEE from a thermos flask, in which case, while you attempt to drink it without suffering THIRD DEGREE BURNS, ask them to steer with one hand.

Mirrors

Throughout any journey, all mirrors should be utilised effectively. Compact mirrors are particularly useful for applying make up, checking that you haven't any TOOTHPASTE AROUND YOUR MOUTH or spinach between your teeth.

OVERTAKING

Only overtake on the outside lane. Using the inside lane is illegal, although this doesn't stop the ever-expanding legion of boy racers from doing so. To be honest, the cars they're driving are probably stolen anyway, so an extra charge of overtaking on the inside lane is hardly going to bother them.

Overtaking large vehicles is very difficult, especially those STRETCH LIMOS that go on forever or oversized juggernauts used in MONSTER TRUCK conventions. As a general rule the longer the vehicle the more time it will take to overtake.

Overtake large vehicles with care, ensuring you don't make eye contact with the driver, as drivers of HGVs are usually bigger than you by the same proportion that their vehicle is bigger than yours.

You **MUST NOT** overtake when:

• **the road you're using is a very narrow dirt track with no passing places**

• **you're on someone's drive**

• **your vehicle is going through a car wash.**

Being overtaken

Being overtaken can be an unpleasant experience. It can be INTIMIDATING and downright RUDE. It can affect your pride, dignity and sense of self. However, if you are being overtaken your response must be measured and sensible – put your foot down and overtake the bastard back, LAUGHING MANIACALLY as you do so and flicking the 'V' sign to all and sundry.

ROAD JUNCTIONS

Overtaking at road junctions is dangerous for pedestrians, so go right ahead and do it.

Box junctions – these are those yellow grids at major junctions and in theory you must not enter one of them unless your road or lane ahead is clear. However, a recent survey has shown this to be the most disobeyed of all road rules – no one, but no one takes a blind bit of notice of it.

Junctions controlled by traffic lights

The white line on the ground beside traffic lights is there for a specific purpose: to stop you. Edging just over the line or brazenly jutting a few feet over it is mere posturing and saying, 'LOOK HOW HARD I AM.'

Turning right

Because we here in Blighty insist on driving on the left, turning right is a bit of a pain. One way of avoiding this manoeuvre is to turn left, left and left again. However, this can be extremely time-consuming, so, when you wish to turn right, pull over to the right-hand side of the road – don't bother letting any other road users know your intentions – and hover hoping that someone in the oncoming traffic will extend you the courtesy of letting you go. They won't. SWEAR and CURSE at every driver who fails to let you turn bearing in mind that when you are in the oncoming traffic you will never extend the same courtesy to someone wanting to turn right.

A car attempting to turn right on a busy road

ROUNDABOUTS

On approaching a roundabout, study the sign by the side of the road that tells you where the LOOMING exits lead. This is not easy as many of them are placed a couple of yards from the roundabout and are thus almost impossible to see. Road planners put these signs there on purpose. Publicly they say this is to check up on whether drivers are fully alert. But in secret, they have confessed that they just do this to have a laugh at CCTV PICTURES OF DRIVERS' CONFUSION.

The nearer you get to a roundabout the more specific the road signs become. What starts off as the A127 becomes Little Totham and ends up as Granny Keeble's house.

Whatever you do, **DO NOT** keep going round in circles. A couple of circuits when working out which exit you wish to take is fine, more than 15 it's best to just give up and admit YOU'RE LOST.

Mini-roundabouts are exactly what their name describes. They are both mini and roundabouts. Don't be tempted to drive right through them even if there are no other vehicles in the vicinity. This action does give the driver a small THRILL OF EXCITEMENT ('Ooh, look at me, I'm driving right through the middle of a mini-roundabout'), but it is a bad habit and can easily lead to other BAD HABITS – such as SLURPING your soup, cheating at SCRABBLE or driving straight across normal roundabouts.

PEDESTRIAN CROSSINGS

DO NOT leave your vehicle parked on a pedestrian crossing. While more sprightly members of the public, irrespective of age, are only too happy to vault over your vehicle or at least walk round it, the less springy members of the community may stand in front of it until you return. If you're on a summer break, this is a lot of waiting.

Zebra crossings were invented by John 'Zebra' Constantinople, an engineer from Dorset. Some black and white pots of paint had fallen off a lorry, onto a road near his home, leaving a zebra-like pattern on the road. As he stood observing this sight, he noticed that every car that approached the pattern, stopped. He then went round to tell his friend Peter 'Belisha Beacon' Guernsey and together they came up with the idea of the crossings we now know and cherish. Both men were awarded knighthoods in 1954. THEY RECENTLY MARRIED.

Signal-controlled crossings

Pelican crossings – for vehicle drivers these are very annoying signal-controlled crossings because they give pedestrians the opportunity to control road traffic. Some MILITANT PEDESTRIANS, not satisfied with this amount of control, walk across the road and then press the button on the other side and walk back, continuing in this way for up to half an hour. In such cases, drivers need to MOUNT the pavement and see how the pedestrians like that.

REVERSING

This means driving backwards and in truth is far harder than driving forwards. However, there are some very important tips to improve one's reversing skills:

• put the gear stick into reverse

• don't exceed the speed limit, especially when on a motorway

• make sure you're alone.

• Reversing, and especially reverse parking, is a hundred times harder when you're being watched.

Non-politically correct people will insist that women cannot reverse, especially into parking spaces. Politically correct people also think this, but won't say it.

Some larger vehicles make a 'reversing noise', a bit like a ROBOT DUCK caught in a mangle, to warn other road users that they are moving backwards. This sound has been recorded and released on a white-label single and has become a HUGE HIT IN IBIZA and at transport cafes.

8. ROAD USERS REQUIRING EXTRA CARE

Particularly vulnerable pedestrians

Teenagers/old people – even though they are chronologically at opposite ends of the spectrum, when it comes to their behaviour as pedestrians they are remarkably similar. In a word, they are slow – really, annoyingly slow – old people out of necessity, teenagers out of a desire to be COOL AND LAID BACK. This is never truer than at a zebra crossing. At a push teenagers will amble across; for the most part they will shuffle. The elderly will treat the other side of the road as the summit of EVEREST and do everything they can to conserve their energy while attempting to reach that point. Shouting at them rarely helps, so the best thing to do is use the time constructively. It might be a good time to do your tax return or attempt to solve a complex QUADRATIC EQUATION.

Mentals/loons/bag people – easy to spot because they'll be wearing 300 shirts, forty-SEVEN PAIRS OF TROUSERS and a STOAT, and be carrying all their worldly possessions in an Asda bag. On the whole they tend not to go anywhere near cars, believing them to be aliens.

INTERESTING FACT

(Animals) Monkeys at Windsor Safari Park have become so good at dismantling cars, some of them have been offered part-time jobs in scrapyards.

Drunks – inebriated people on the streets will go through the same stages of drunkenness as they do in a pub. So, initially, they will think that all cars are their best mates and try to cuddle them. They'll then become very TEARFUL and weep on people's bonnets, creating rust problems, before finally offering out a lamp-post for looking at them funny and HEAD-BUTTING it.

Protestors – if you find yourself stuck behind a protest march, find out what it is they're protesting about; if you agree with the theme of their protest, drive slowly behind them; if, however, you disagree, PLOUGH ON THROUGH THEM, unless you happen to be driving a tank through Tiananmen Square in China and the world's press is watching. In this case, stop and let the protestor carry out his protest making sure to get a good look at him so you can TORTURE him at a later stage.

INTERESTING FACT
(Roadworks) The world's longest diversion was in India on the road between Delhi and Calcutta. Drivers were guided off the road in to neighbouring Bangladesh and then returned via Nepal and Bhutan. Needless to say none of them made it.

A gang of those-little-electric-cart-jackers ⟩⟩

Elderly drivers

In cars – elderly people driving cars fall into two categories; those who think they're driving at the speed of light, but are in fact barely moving, and those who are in fact driving at the SPEED OF LIGHT, but think they're barely moving. It's not worth taking issue with them as they'll get very irate and say something about having fought in TWO WORLD WARS.

Old people in those little electric carts – these are the elderly and infirms' equivalent of the very latest skateboard or roller blade. They're highly sought after, especially among the doubly INCONTINENT, gangs of whom are largely responsible for the recent spate of those-little-electric-cart-jackings. Care should be taken when driving past them due to the frequency with which COLOSTOMY BAGS are jettisoned.

Learner drivers

We were all learner drivers once, so you'd think we'd have more sympathy for those under instruction. Sadly this is not the case and, if caught behind a learner, the correct procedure is to get incredibly frustrated with how slowly they're driving, shout 'get off the road', honk your horn repeatedly and, when you finally get past, FLICK THEM THE FINGER.

New drivers – in recent years, drivers who have just passed their test have taken to putting a 'P'-plate on their cars to signify just that. Sadly, just as with an L-plate, this makes SOD ALL difference and, if they're still driving like a learner, they can expect the same treatment as above.

Other road users

Really big vehicles will invariably be blocking the road by trying to reverse out of a space just big enough for a skateboard. Whatever you do, don't vent your frustration by shouting or honking your horn; the driver will step down from his cab, give you a mouthful and then have a lengthy read of *The Sun* or *Architecture Today*, before resuming reversing.

Dustcarts – whenever you try and take a cheeky shortcut one of two things happens – you get caught in a MAZE OF ONE-WAY ROADS or you turn into a quiet road, an as yet fantastically undiscovered cut-through, only to be met with

ing freely, oh no, hang on …

the back end of a dustcart agonisingly slowly
making its way down the street. Before you have
time to reverse, a number of other cars have
appeared behind you making your 'short' cut
a very long cut.

Taxis – be wary of them performing random
U-turns and pulling over suddenly if they get
the slightest whiff of a fare.

Coaches – unless taking a group of
PENSIONERS FROM THE WOMEN'S GUILD to
a crocheting conference, be prepared to be
mooned at whenever driving behind a coach.
However, be PREPARED TO BE MOONED at
when driving behind a coach taking a group of
pensioners back from a Women's Guild
crocheting conference – after a couple of swift
sherries, these octogenarians can get quite frisky
and the sight of an 85-year-old's ARSE
splattered across a coach window can be quite
upsetting for some motorists.

Emergency vehicles rushing to an emergency
– get out of their way, but then, as soon as
they've gone past, start following them as
closely as you can; it's by far the quickest way to
get anywhere.

Police cars not rushing to an emergency –
slow down to the speed limit until you're past
them, THEN PUT YOUR FOOT DOWN.

Rollerbladers – really annoying fuckers who
have no right to be on the road. Make no
allowances – MOW THEM DOWN.

9. DRIVING IN ADVERSE WEATHER CONDITIONS

This section is concerned with the sort of conditions that, when you look out of the window before you set off on a journey, make you say, 'Oh bloody hell, look at that. I'll never get there. I think I'll stay in and watch subtitled repeats of 'BLESS THIS HOUSE' on UK Gold.'

Rain

Light – during a light shower it is advisable to set your windscreen wipers to 'intermittent'. If your vehicle doesn't have this setting, you can give the impression that it does by switching your wipers on and off every five seconds.

Medium – during a medium shower, get out of the car and cover it with washing up liquid. You'll save a fortune on car washes.

Really pissing down – this is the sort of rain whereby it seems as if someone is sitting on the roof and pouring buckets of water over your windscreen. Safety is paramount in these conditions. Under no circumstances should you open the windows – you will drown unless you have professional SCUBA DIVING equipment in the car. It's also essential to deal with the reality of the situation – don't sit back and imagine that you are on a sun-kissed beach in the Caribbean. You're not. You're on the A12, the kids are screaming, you won't be home before midnight and all you have to eat until then is a six-pack of FRUESLI BARS and some QUAVERS.

However, to lighten the mood, it is permissible to laugh at pedestrians caught in the downpour.

Overtaking an articulated lorry – doing this in heavy rain is HIGHLY DANGEROUS. As you draw alongside the lorry the spray combined with the actual rain will pound your car, forcing you to push it ever harder to get through the wall of water. Your vehicle will be buffeted to and fro, your every synapse stretched to bursting point as you fight to keep control of your car. SWEAT WILL DRIP FROM EVERY PORE OF YOUR BODY, creating yet more water for you to cope with. Your life will flash before your eyes as great TORRENTS OF WATER THRASH against the body of your car – like water DEMONS clawing to drag you to a liquidy death. Eventually, if you're lucky, you will emerge, as a baby from a particularly difficult water birth, taking great gulps of air and thanking the good Lord above that you're still alive. IT'S FUCKING GREAT.

INTERESTING FACT
(Waiting and parking) Cars that run on lead free petrol are no easier to park than other cars.

Ice and snow

Gauging how icy it is – if, before you set off on your journey, you look out of a window and see a woman in a short skirt performing a credible triple salko, it's pretty bad.

Forecast – always listen to the weather forecast before setting out. If no snow is predicted, be prepared for snow. It's remarkable how often they get it wrong, is it not?

Black ice – black ice cannot be seen, but apparently it is there, a bit like God.

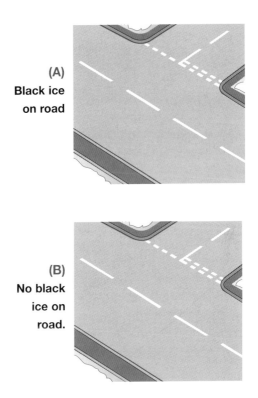

(A)
Black ice
on road

(B)
No black
ice on
road.

Gritters – even though it happens without fail every single year, local councils remain totally unprepared for ice and snow. Consequently the gritting will only happen once everything has melted, making road conditions worse. Don't be fooled by those huge yellow bins that seem to MIRACULOUSLY appear at roadsides in extreme weather conditions, bearing the word 'GRIT'. These generally contain NO GRIT WHATSOEVER, and are just a means of the council spending their yearly budget.

Wind

Hurricanes, gales, twisters – defined in the UK by someone saying, 'Ooh, it's a bit blowy out' – can make driving conditions hazardous and you might experience the sensation known as 'being buffeted about' in your car. However, if the wind is in your favour and you have a large sail you can erect on the roof of your car, you'll arrive at your destination far more quickly.

In windy conditions if you keep all windows shut you should not experience the gusts inside your vehicle. If you do, you've left the air conditioning on.

Other weather conditions

Fog – to aid visibility use your fog lights. If visibility gets down to 5 metres you can also use a foghorn. If visibility drops to zero metres, park and rest up with a thermos flask of coffee and a FAMILY-SIZED BAG OF MINSTRELS. Cover yourself in old newspapers or leaves.

Hot weather – there never used to be any rules pertaining to hot weather in the UK as there never used to be any hot weather. However, due to global warming that has all changed, so here are some tips:

• **There is no need** to think you are going blind – your vision is not blurred, it is merely heat haze on the road.

- **Hosepipe ban** – this only applies to using them, it is still permitted to have one in the car.

- **Air conditioning** – guaranteed to break down on the hottest day in living memory.

Earthquakes – if the earth in front opens up into a GAPING, BOTTOMLESS PIT, take a detour, making sure you avoid any deranged, wandering refugees made homeless by the quake.

Volcanic eruptions – molten lava can be really annoyingly difficult to drive through, even in a 4x4.

10. WAITING AND PARKING

Trying to find a parking space has become a national obsession thanks to the ever-increasing resident-permit-only streets and the number of cars on the road. The situation has got so bad, that in some cases when drivers actually do find a space (even if it's miles from where they live) rather than give it up, they will leave their car there forever and buy a house, GET A JOB and find a school for their children in that area.

A number of drivers are coached intensely to park, but only in micro cars. Some drivers lose the ability to park the second they pass their driving test. This is a fault of our EXAM-BASED CULTURE and requires deeper discussion in a far more wide-ranging way than is possible here.

You **MUST NOT** wait or park:

- **On single or double yellow lines.** However, as the law says nothing about waiting <u>and</u> parking, you could try sitting in your car on a single or double yellow line and having it out with the traffic warden when he or she attempts to give you a ticket. The resulting legal battle to have the law clarified will be well worth all your time and effort, even if it does cost you your life savings and leave you DESTITUTE.

- **In the space across your street** that's always used by the huge threatening guy who drives the exhaustless WHITE VAN.

PARKING

Use off-street parking areas. These are growing increasingly rare. In some areas there is absolutely no off-street parking. This is down to a desire by local councils to get more people to use public transport. However, in areas where bus and train services are poor, some people end up not being able to get anywhere at any time, other than by walking. For distances of under 3 miles this is acceptable. For any distance over this, training is needed and can only be given by a qualified OLYMPIC SPEED-WALKER. As a result of this lack of off-street parking, some homeowners are renting out their driveways as parking spaces and in one case as an art studio.

Lock your vehicle unless you want it to be stolen. In this case leave all of the doors open, the keys in the ignition, the engine running and a large sign on the front windscreen stating

'TAKE THIS BLOODY THING OFF MY HANDS'.

As a note of caution, insurance companies have got wind of these scams and have started sending their workers out into the streets. You can always uncover them though by shouting, 'LOWER PREMIUMS PLEASE!'

You **MUST NOT** stop or park on

- bicycles

- bus stops

- setting concrete

- traffic wardens
      (no matter how tempting it might be).

TAURUS CAR (bought between 21 April – 21 May)
Pluto in Jupiter in Saturn in Mars means it's a good day for luck.
Park wherever you like, even on a zigzag.

Controlled parking zones

These are a bugger and their messages are OFTEN CONFUSED. Some forbid you from parking in a bay for a specific time period during the day – for example, don't park here between 3.05 a.m. and 2.16 a.m., while others require a resident's permit in order to park within their confines. These permits are like gold dust and cannot be claimed on the basis that you're going to be resident in that area for two hours while you go shopping.

The officials who police these zones are trained at a specialist CRACK OPERATIVE TRAFFIC WARDEN CENTRE in the Norfolk Broads. The councils/companies who employ these officials sometimes offer prizes based on how many tickets an individual can issue. This can get confusing, as one of their number discovered when he issued seventeen hundred tickets – all to the same vehicle – and then claimed his trip to Mauritius. The driver of the vehicle receiving this ONSLAUGHT OF TICKETS launched a massive court case against the council in question, because the tickets prevented him from seeing out of his front mirror, forcing him to crash into the parking ticket department of that very local council.

Goods vehicles

Loading and unloading

There is a myriad of rules and laws that apply to parking when loading or unloading goods (oh alright then, there's three):

• **Park as near to the goods'** final destination as possible – do not park 14 miles from the house you're delivering a new kitchen to.

• **After parking,** leave your vehicle and go to the nearest café for a well-deserved three-hour lunch. Similarly, after unloading one item, stop and have a FORTY-MINUTE TEA BREAK. (Repeat after each item.)

• **To be certain of a parking space** near to the house receiving the goods, ask the owner to 'bagsy' or reserve a space by putting three wheelie bins in the road directly outside | their house.

Parking at night

Parking at night is far more difficult than parking during the day. And this isn't just because the light is worse. There are so many more distractions for the driver at night, such as discothèques, late-night garages and pubs with THEMED KARAOKE NIGHTS.

<<< **The work of an over-zealous Mauritius-bound traffic warden**

Parking on hills

If you park on a hill you should:

Put the handbrake on, leave the car in reverse or first gear depending on whether you're facing up or down the hill, put bricks under each wheel and tie the door handle to the nearest lamppost.

Take in your surroundings – hills can be places of natural beauty.

Hill starts

The legendary 'hill start' is a remarkably difficult manoeuvre to master. As one sees daily, there are an entire slew of drivers who have not perfected this skill. How many times has the car in front of you at traffic lights on a hill slid back several metres, almost crashing into your vehicle? Indeed, so frequent has this occurrence become that there is a MUSHROOMING CAMPAIGN to alter radically this country's driving test, making hill starts the sole focus of the exam. The other skills like steering etc., would be passed on trust.

Parking when others are watching you

For men this is the ULTIMATE TEST OF MASCULINITY. Even if it's just a glance from a disinterested dog-walker or their dog, the parking must be executed with STYLE and PANACHE. Failure to do so will result in ones' masculinity being questioned.

d when stuck in traffic for hours.'

If the parking space is too small

Either buy another vehicle or leave your car jutting out outrageously into the road. As you walk along the street and look back to check your car you experience two simultaneous sensations: first, you feel like a suave, JAMES DEAN figure, to whom a parking space means nothing. Second, you feel your bowels turn to water as the clamping and towing away lorry appears out of nowhere.

If you scratch another unoccupied car

This is one of the most HOTLY DEBATED aspects of CAR-PARKING ETIQUETTE, to leave a note or to scarper? In most cases the appropriate action is to leave an apologetic note bearing the name and details of someone you particularly dislike.

Pay & Display car parks

Technically these should be called simply 'Display' car parks as paying is part of the procedure involved in parking in any car park. At one time they were great examples of how the HUMAN SPIRIT OF KINDNESS will always triumph, as people would offer others their ticket if leaving before the time on that ticket had expired. However, this practice has been clamped down on, as you are now required to enter your number-plate details when purchasing a ticket, thus proving that the HUMAN SPIRIT OF BEING ABSOLUTE BASTARDS will always triumph.

Underground / Multi-storey car parks

These are very expensive, poorly lit, badly ventilated and underground. It is very easy to get lost in these LABYRINTHINE CONCRETE MONSTROSITIES and drive round and round in figures of eight (or infinity if you prefer). It is also extremely common to forget exactly where it was you parked your car. In this instance it is advisable to place a 10-metre, flashing, multi-coloured pylon on the roof of your vehicle to alert you to its presence.

Another rule of thumb is NOT to get involved in AN ARGUMENT with the people at the electronic barrier gates. The people who operate these gates are taught to use a lexicon consisting of a mere ten words. So do not be shocked when they respond to you testing to see if they have a SENSE OF HUMOUR by asking, 'Is destruction of the environment or the advance of DIALECTIC MATERIALISM, the greatest threat facing humankind?' by saying, 'ONE POUND FIFTY'.

INTERESTING FACT

(Roundabouts) The largest roundabout in the world is in Bolivia. It has a circumference of 14 miles, a fully operational power station on its central reservation and 36 exits.

Two selfish parkers getting their just deserts

Selfish parkers

These are people who when they see a space big enough for two cars will park right in the middle of it, thus denying other drivers the chance to take advantage of the space. If you see someone parking like this, follow them home, enter their house and lie right in the middle of their TWO-SEATER SOFA, forcing them to perch on the edge of a very sharp-cornered coffee table.

73

The space mirage

A curse of the modern world, this describes a situation, where a car/van driver sees a parking space from a distance and celebrates JOYFULLY, until they reach the actual 'space' and discover that a motorbike is already parked there.

Remembering where you have parked

Always make a point of remembering where you have parked your car. Returning to the wrong place and assuming your car has been stolen because it is not there will lead to SEVERE EMBARRASSMENT and may result in you being ostracised by your core friendship group.

GEMINI CAR (bought between 22 May – 22 June)
A work opportunity beckons. You'll become a cab.

11. MOTORWAYS AND SERVICE STATIONS

Driving on the motorway can be hazardous; keeping your foot hard down on the accelerator for hours on end can often make your ankle quite STIFF AND SORE, but for most of us it's the closest we come to Formula 1 racing, so it's a small price to pay.

GENERAL

Fuel

About 60 miles prior to joining any motorway, you will notice that every petrol station you pass will have a sign proclaiming 'Last chance to fill up before motorway'. This is a LIE perpetuated by the owners so that they can charge EXORBITANT PRICES for their fuel and sundries (though not quite as stratospherically exorbitant as the PRICES charged by motorway service stations).

INTERESTING FACT

(Traffic jams) The Hungarian word for traffic jam is 'Ekérem segítsen' which, literally translated means, 'traffic marmalade'.

Children

Unless absolutely necessary, do not take children on motorway journeys. Within nanoseconds of starting your journey they will repeat the following three sentences ad infinitum: 'I want to get out', 'I NEED A WEE', 'Are we there yet?' If left uncurtailed, this constant babble will cause the driver to go BERSERK and repeatedly threaten to turn around and go home, something they have absolutely no intention of doing.

DRIVING ON THE MOTORWAY

Joining the motorway

You usually join a motorway via a slip road. In order to do so you should:

Wait for a suitable gap in the traffic before attempting to pull out. The average waiting time in EU countries is forty-five minutes.

If no bastard lets you out, pull out anyway. The parallel vehicle will swerve into the next lane to avoid you and, as you are ahead of them, the resulting accident and 15-MILE TAILBACK will not affect you.

Leaving the motorway

Ideally when leaving the motorway you should move into the slow lane in good time and then indicate left before exiting. In practice, you will find yourself doing 90 in the fast lane and be almost past the junction you need when you realise what's happened, shout 'OH SHIT, I'M MEANT TO GET OFF HERE' and pull across three lanes, mounting the soft verge in the process.

Middle-lane hogger

This describes a person who, when driving from, say, London to Inverness will spend the entire motorway section of the journey in the middle lane, not budging for anything, even an EARTHQUAKE. When confronted with such a driver it is permissible to overtake them in any way possible; for example, use the fast lane, slow lane, hard shoulder, other side of the motorway or use a FLYING CAR (but you will have to wait until 2058 to do this).

How to deal with middle-lane hoggers – pull back in front of them really, really closely so that they have to BREAK VIOLENTLY. Don't forget to gesticulate wildly the whole time.

INTERESTING FACT
(Adverse weather conditions) A recent survey discovered that 4 out of 13 people would rather drive in sleet than in hail.

Service station etiquette

Service stations are mysterious places. Several are so disconnected (physically, emotionally and spiritually) from the rest of the country that they have declared themselves as INDEPENDENT TERRITORIES – and have been recognised as such by the United Nations.

The fact that service stations are mysterious is predominantly due to the following fact – even though all types and classes of people drive on motorways, when it comes to service stations, only the worst type of CHAV RIFF-RAFF seem to inhabit them. If, however, you do find yourself in one, the following guidelines apply:

Because of the disgraceful pricing regimes of these establishments it is advisable to bring your own sandwiches and eat them provocatively – centimetres away from the faces of service station staff.

You may picnic on the grass verges behind the car park. If, however, you view this as the ideal picnic location, please seek psychiatric help immediately.

When leaving a service station you will often encounter hitchhikers. Prior to 1982, when they were predominantly STUDENTS or HIPPIES, it was acceptable to pick them up. Now that they are all homicidal maniacs you should ACCELERATE WILDLY or

RUN THEM OVER.

A hitchiker
prior to 1982 >>>

A hitchiker after 1982

Traffic jams

When driving on a motorway:

Never, ever say, 'The roads aren't bad today, we're making good time.' If you do say this sentence, then within two minutes you will be BUMPER TO BUMPER with the other cars on the motorway and moving at 3 miles an hour.

When stuck in a jam,whichever lane you are in will be the slowest moving. Switching lanes is pointless, as any lane that appears to be moving faster than the one you're in will instantly GRIND TO A HALT as soon as you move into it.

MOTORWAY TRAFFIC JAMS END FOR NO APPARENT REASON.

Hard shoulder

You are only permitted to stop on the hard shoulder for one reason:

TO LET A YOUNG CHILD DEFECATE.

Motorway speed limits

The national speed limit is 70 miles per hour. On motorways, the national speed limit is 70 miles per hour. See the difference? That's right, it was a trick question; there is no difference. However, there is the widely known UNWRITTEN RULE that it is acceptable to do 80, 90 or even 100 mph on Britain's motorways, unless there is a police car in the vicinity, in which case all traffic slows down to 70 mph and then speeds up again to 80, 90 or 100 mph when well past the police car.

12. BREAKDOWNS AND ACCIDENTS

BREAKDOWNS

Signs that your vehicle has broken down are

- it's not moving, but you want it to

- the lights on the dashboard resemble a Santa's grotto with dodgy wiring

- there are no more and no less than three simultaneous explosions from the engine

- the car is engulfed in flames

What to do when your vehicle breaks down

You can cry, scream or if American, holler, but unless you have a speaker phone directly connected to a motoring organisation, your cries, screams or if American, hollers will remain unanswered. No one, but no one will stop to help you.

Do **NOT** stand beside your vehicle. It is better to stand by the roadside calmly. If you are an EXCITABLE INDIVIDUAL, then you may stand on top of your vehicle.

If your vehicle experiences problems on a motorway, pull over on to the hard shoulder, making sure you don't over run into a field bearing a giant advertising sign for 'KOI CARP IN 2 MILES' or 'Boot Sale Here Every Sunday'.

Obstructions

If anything falls from another vehicle do not stop to pick it up. This does not apply to situations where the fallen load is plasma TV SCREENS or EXPENSIVE SWISS WATCHES where it is advisable to stop and collect as many as possible, even if they've fallen off in the middle of a six-lane motorway. When you come to FLOG THEM DOWN THE PUB you can genuinely say, hand on heart, that they 'fell off the back of a lorry'.

Emergency phones

Try and stop near to a roadside emergency telephone. These should be no more than a mile apart from each other. These phones link directly to the police and breakdown companies. You cannot use them to connect to PREMIUM-RATE SEX CHAT LINES.

CANCER CAR (bought between 23 June – 23 July)
Your relationship is suffering because you're moving too fast; put the brakes on and slow down.

Dealing with the police

For a fast response tell them you are a woman travelling alone; you have always respected the constabulary; or want to become a police officer yourself – a recruiting sergeant is always at hand. When an officer arrives and sees that you are in fact a 6-foot, 25-stone BEARDED MALE, you can dispense with the falsetto voice, the game will be up.

Breakdown companies

If a man is driving, but there's a woman in the car, she'll suggest calling the AA, the RAC or Green Flag the moment the car breaks down. The man will say no, spend an hour under the bonnet and then suggest calling the AA, the RAC or Green Flag.

At any given service station, be it day or night, there will always be a representative from one or other of the breakdown companies offering you VARIOUS ENTICEMENTS to join their organisations. Recent enticements include the complete set of the 1978 edition of the *Encyclopaedia Britannica* and a subscription to CANAL BOATS MONTHLY.

Rejoining the carriageway

Once your vehicle is ready to drive again, you must be extra careful when rejoining the carriageway. When you're stuck on the hard shoulder, you can see first hand that 'cars go bloody quickly on the motorway'. It is necessary to build up speed on the hard shoulder first, but don't take this to extremes. Some drivers stay on the hard shoulder until the end of the motorway, doing over 100 mph and CACKLING MADLY at all of the vehicles they are overtaking.

Mechanics

If your car can make it to the end of your motorway journey but needs attention, take it to the most REPUTABLE LOCAL MECHANIC. Once upon a time mechanics had a bad name for overstating problems and hiking up their quotes and prices. They prayed on the WANTON IGNORANCE of the general public in all things car-mechanic-related. However, today's 'new' mechanics are fair and will attempt to get your car back to you before it broke down. (If you believe that, you'll believe anything.)

ACCIDENTS

When passing an accident on the other side of the motorway, it is customary to slow down and take a long, voyeuristic look at the CARNAGE. However, this practice can lead to you not concentrating on your own steering skills and having a crash yourself. If this happens, the motorists on the other side of the motorway who are already slowing down because of the crash on their side, will slow down even more to look at the crash on your side – probably resulting in one of them having a crash on their side. In extreme situations this can lead to **UNENDING GRIDLOCK**.

DO NOT get involved with any injured passengers for the following reasons:

First Aid is not like in the movies; SANDRA BULLOCK will not suddenly appear to pass you bandages, nor will TOM HANKS pass you an air cushion.

MOST INJURED PEOPLE WON'T WANT TO DATE YOU.

'So, what are you doing next Saturday?'

Calmly lead uninjured passengers off the motorway by shrieking at the top of your voice, 'GET OUT OF THE WAY YOU IDIOT! There's been an accident.'

Accidents involving dangerous goods

Any vehicle carrying dangerous loads is marked with orange hazard-warning plates. In cases such as these get the hell out of there. HIGHLY TOXIC WASTE and POISONOUS CHEMICALS are unpleasant to the touch.

Whenever one hears on the radio about a dangerous lorry involved in a motorway incident, the word 'JACK-KNIFED' is always used. This term doesn't actually mean anything; it is just in the 'Radio reporters' handbook of flash words to throw at the public to show them that they're not as clever as radio reporters'.

Documentation

If you are involved in an accident in any way then it's important that you have certain documents with you, including your car registration number and your insurance certificate. SUPERMARKET LOYALTY CARDS are not acceptable.

> LEO CAR (bought between 24 July – 23 August)
> Love comes along in the form of a 1978 Blue Ford Fiesta with a slight dent in its rear fender.

13. ROADWORKS

Ironically, roads don't work when there are roadworks being carried out on their surfaces but, frustrating as they can be, this maintenance of the highways and byways is essential if the highways and byways are to be maintained. On the whole, most roadwork contractors will go out of their way to ensure that any DISRUPTION TO YOUR JOURNEY is kept to a maximum.

No one really knows where roadworks come from – the phenomenon of waking up in the morning to discover roadworks outside your house, otherwise known as Spontaneous Roadwork Construction (or SRC), is universal and as mysterious as the unexplained instances of CROP CIRCLE APPEARANCE. Roadworks seem to mysteriously appear, usually on a Sunday morning, in what was a hitherto quiet and peaceful street. Many theories abound as to how they get there, though the current favourite, that people come and put them up in the night, is as yet unproven.

For some reason the traditional sign for 'roadworks ahead' depicts a man hard at work, however, there are calls for a more accurate representation

Go/Stop sign – where roadworks cause a restriction in the flow of traffic, temporary traffic lights will be ERECTED or a man holding a sign with 'Go' on one side and 'Stop' on the other will perform the function of a traffic light. However, in the latter case, if the man is not relieved after half an hour, the power will start to go to his head. In a KING CANUTE type of way, he will stop traffic and let it go at his behest. In certain cases men have been known to favour the traffic flow from one direction for vast periods of time, only letting the contra-directional traffic through when they have bestowed upon him many fine gifts such as silk, gems, TURTLES DOVES and CRUNCHIE BARS.

Diversions – diversions will never lead you back to where you want to go. Furthermore, after sending you hither and thither down many a back alley, the signs will dwindle and then disappear altogether leaving you utterly lost. The best thing to do is DO WHAT THEY DO IN FILMS. Drive as fast as you can towards the roadworks making sure that just before you reach them you drive over an object that is resting at a 45-degree angle to the ground in order to lift you over the roadworks with a view to landing safely on the other side and continuing on your journey.

Pneumatic drills – these fall into the same category as car alarms; they produce one of the most annoying sounds known to humankind. They are always used in close proximity to people with HANGOVERS, night workers trying to rest and young babies who have just dropped off to sleep.

Roadworks on motorways

Cones set out on motorways to cordon off roadworks will always be placed unnecessarily far away from where the actual work is meant to be taking place, bottle-necking and slowing traffic to a virtual standstill up to ten miles away from the actual roadworks.

Roadwork warning signs

These signs are usually put up several months (and in some cases, years) before roadworks are due to take place and say things like, 'On 16 October for nineteen weeks this road will become a COMPLETE NIGHTMARE, with traffic slowed down to 2 mph and causing substantial and elongated periods of road rage. We apologise for any inconvenience this may cause.'

VIRGO CAR (bought between 24th August – 23rd September)
Your owner's been feeling very tense lately, but don't worry, it's because of money worries, so he can't afford to buy a new car.

14. RAILWAY LEVEL CROSSINGS

A level crossing is where a railway line crosses a road and ironically, because of that very fact, it is not actually level. It is obviously not sensible to park on a level crossing when a train is HURTLING DOWN THE TRACK TOWARDS YOU AT 120 MPH, however, an exception can be made when it's a toy train on a vast Hornby track set up in someone's attic (the type of attics you can only access by way of a terribly dangerous ladder that sometimes crashes down from its moorings on the ceiling for no apparent reason).

The other crucial factor about railway level crossings is that no matter how infrequently trains run, how late trains may be and how much STRIKE ACTION the railway staff take, there will always be a train coming when you approach the crossing causing you to sit in a traffic jam. This is an irrefutable fact of SOD'S LAW.

Similarly, as you sit in your car watching the train hurtle by, you will look jealously at all the passengers having a restful and speedy journey and make a MENTAL NOTE to take the train next time. However, when next time comes your train will be SEVERELY DELAYED because of strike action and leaves on the line and, as you sit in your stationary carriage looking out to all the fast-moving traffic on the road, you will make a mental note to drive your car next time and WEEP LIKE A LITTLE GIRL.

Controlled crossings

Calling a crossing controlled is stating the bleeding obvious somewhat, as one would hope that all crossings are controlled otherwise you will simply sit in your car for hours waiting for it to open. (Hang on a minute ...)

You **MUST NEVER** drive across a level crossing and then reverse back across it and then go forwards again and so on playing a form of speeding-train Russian roulette unless you are undecided about COMMITTING SUICIDE or not, in which case it's a great way to let fate help you make the decision.

You **MUST** wait if a train goes by and the warning light stays on. This can mean one of two things:

- another train is coming

- the signal operator died shortly after the warning light was activated.

Accidents and breakdowns

If for any reason your vehicle actually breaks down on the crossing, then get yourself and your passengers out as quickly as possible. Ridiculous gentlemanly etiquette is, although polite, best avoided.

If it's possible to push your vehicle off the crossing then do so, though if it's insured for a decent sum of MONEY and you fancy a new car, take a safe position, some distance from the track, and wait for the IMPACT.

15. TRAMWAYS

Trams were extremely popular in the 1880s but fell out of favour and were phased out in 1920 on account of them being unnecessary and not as good as buses or cars. Three years later everyone said, 'Weren't trams GREAT?' so they were promptly reintroduced. In 1963 it dawned on people that they were unnecessary and not as good as buses or cars, so they were phased out. Three years later someone said, 'Weren't trams GREAT?' so, in 1966, they were reintroduced. Thirty years later, in 1996, they were phased out for reasons similar to those given above. In 1999, however, they were reintroduced for reasons similar to those given above. The last tram was seen in the UK in 2005 but there is strong pressure to reintroduce them because they were apparently GREAT.

INTERESTING FACT

(Breakdowns and accidents) Even if a car crashes in to another car on purpose, it will still be referred to as an 'accident.

16. LIGHT SIGNALS CONTROLLING TRAFFIC

Motorway signals

A sign informing you that a lane is closed will appear long before the actual lane closure starts giving you plenty of time to move over into an open lane. However, you won't in fact move over into the open lane until the last possible minute believing that the longer you stay in the closed lane, the quicker your journey will be. This is a fallacy because when you try and move over into the open lane, none of the cars in it will let you do so, thus adding considerable time to your journey and MAKING YOU FEEL LIKE A:

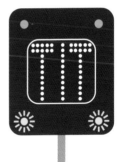

Should you see a sign like the one below on the motorway you might be tempted to think, 'OK, 50's not too bad, it's probably just the SHEER VOLUME OF TRAFFIC, I'm sure once things have cleared a bit we'll be back to 70.' Don't. As sure as eggs is eggs it will be followed by a sign saying '40'. Then '30' and so on until before you know it, you're stationary on a four-lane motorway at the end of a 16-MILE TAILBACK, wishing you'd turned off when you saw the '50' sign and taken an A road.

Traffic light signals

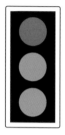
RED means '**Stop**' unless the light has just turned red, in which case it means 'FLOOR YOUR VEHICLE and get through as quickly as possible'. So really it means '**GO**'.

RED AND AMBER technically also means 'Stop', but anyone who has been driving for more than three seconds will know that the moment amber appears you HIT THE ACCELERATOR, effectively making RED AND AMBER mean '**GO**'.

AMBER means 'put your FOOT DOWN and DRIVE LIKE BUGGERY to get through the lights'. So really it means '**GO**'.

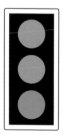
GREEN means '**GO**'. If you're having one of those rare days where every set of lights you approach is turning green, sail through them with a HUGE SMIRK on your face as you glance to the POOR BASTARDS stuck at the lights to your left and right.

Flashing red lights

Alternately flashing red lights mean you must stop and go to the nearest red light district as quickly as possible. The police are in the middle of a clean-up campaign and if you don't get there and distract them soon, they'll arrest all the PROSTITUTES and they'll be none left for when we, I mean, people need them.

INTERESTING FACT
(Motorway) The word 'motorway' comes from the word, 'motor' meaning 'motor' and 'way' meaning 'way'.

17. SIGNALS TO OTHER ROAD USERS

Direction indicator signals

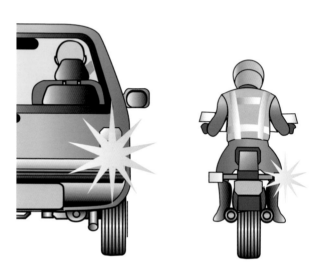

I intend to TURN RIGHT or move out to the right or I may be about to make some sort of manoeuvre to the right, but I may have forgotten that my indicator is on, thus GIVING YOU NO IDEA as to my what my real intentions are.

I intend to turn left or move in to the left or
I MAY BE LOST and looking for a road, so
at the last second I could continue straight on.

I haven't got a clue what I'm going to do,
KEEP WELL AWAY.

Hand, arm and leg signals

'I intend to slow down' OR I'm DRYING MY NAILS.

LIBRA CAR (bought between 24 September – 23 October)
Libra is an air sign, so, if you're feeling a bit flat, it might
be a good idea to check your tyres.

I'm transporting a mannequin or a DEAD BODY and one of its arms is sticking out of the window.

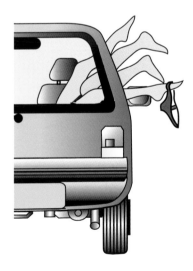

I won't be going anywhere for a little while.

Flashes

Flashing your headlights when driving is a complex signal. Exactly the same action can mean something completely different depending on the context. It is well worth studying the myriad of meanings, because mistaking 'Oh go on then, you go first', for 'FUCK OFF OUT OF IT' can be a lot more than simply embarrassing.

The red car has pulled over to let the brown car pass

In this instance flashed headlights are an act of politeness and kindness, and mean 'after you'. Do not be tempted to flash back a thank you straight away because it may well be taken as a 'no, no, after you'. You will then either both set off at the same time and get stuck or the first car will flash its headlights again, this time meaning 'no, no, really, after you, I insist', in which case you could be CAUGHT IN A GAME of who can be the most polite, akin to arguing over whether or not to go 'Dutch' over a restaurant bill.

The brown car has accepted the red car's 'After you!' and is moving off

Flashing headlights in this case mean 'thank you'. Usually the other car does not flash its headlights back, but if it does, the following interaction can sometimes transpire:

second car returns flash – You're welcome.

first car flashes again – What are you doing later?

second car flashes again – Nothing. Why?

first car flashes again – Fancy getting together tonight at the car wash?

second car flashes again – Yeah, all right.

The car behind wants to get past the car in front so the flashed headlights mean 'Please could you move over so that I can pass?'
if the car in front does not move over, **a second flash means** 'Please could you get out of the way.' **A third flash means** 'Bloody get out of the way.' **A fourth flash means** 'FUCK OFF OUT OF IT!' **Fifth flashes are extremely rare**, but if they do occur it usually means that they are about to **RUN YOU OFF THE ROAD**.

In the previous illustration, the car in the middle lane is allowing the car in the slow lane to pull out in front of it, so effectively the flash means 'GO ON SON, ON YOU GO.' Saying thank you in this case is usually accomplished by the vehicle that has pulled out of the slow lane turning its hazard lights on or, if that vehicle is a lorry, by flicking on the right indicator, then the left indicator and then the right one again. Saying thank you by turning round, facing the car that let you out and flashing your headlights is not advisable.

This flash is specific to night-time driving and means 'TURN YOUR FUCKING LIGHTS DOWN – YOU'RE BLINDING ME.'

Another night-time flash, this one means
'TURN YOUR FUCKING LIGHTS ON.'

In this instance the simplest meaning of the flash is 'Hello.' However, this short-lived pleasantry is often followed by the two HGV or bus drivers stopping alongside each other and the drivers blocking the road by LEANING OUT OF THEIR WINDOWS FOR A CHAT. This can sometimes last long enough for passengers in the vehicles behind to alight, have a three-course meal and grab a game of squash at the local leisure centre before returning to the vehicle.

This very rare instance of vehicle/pedestrian communication means 'You may cross.' A simple wave of the hand will suffice as a thank you. It is not necessary for the pedestrians to produce a pair of car headlights and flash a 'thank you' back.

Carjacking sigals

'Hi, I'm your friendly neighbourhood carjacker. This car I'm currently driving is shit, I'd much rather be driving yours. Can I have it please?' The correct answer in this instance is always 'Yes.'

18. TRAFFIC SIGNS

Signs with red circles are mostly prohibitive.

Signs with blue circles, but no red border mostly give positive instruction, but are not very stylish.

Rectangular signs in green lace with matching pink surround are nice, but SO LAST YEAR.

Triangular signs in purple velvet with yellow and brown trim and a lacquered finish are to die for.

Road sign in 4 miles.

Speed limit 30, but you can get away with 35, as long as you don't push it.

If you can read this
you're too bloody
close

If you can read this you're too bloody close.

Use of modern cameras prohibited.

No undertaking.

You've just missed your turning, sucker!

Conceal all loose change – windscreen washers at next traffic lights.

Very specific sign which applies only to John Maddox.

Sign giving the average IQ scores of inhabitants living in these cities.

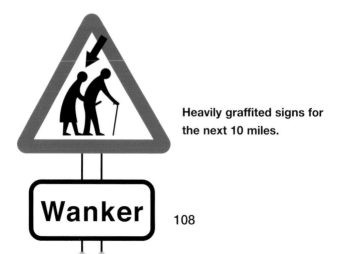

Heavily graffited signs for the next 10 miles.

108

You are an evil person
You must repent or you and
the next seventeen generations
of your family will be punished

A sign from God.

Sign of the times.

The golf club that will
appear in five minutes
uses a code of positive
discrimination – positively
discriminating in favour
of white, middle-aged,
wealthy, straight men.

Delays possible
until
March 2007

Delays probable until September 2008.

19. ROAD MARKINGS

Along the edge of the carriageway

Single yellow line – might be worth taking a chance and parking here, but if some bastard traffic warden does come along you're going to get a ticket.

Double yellow line – you'd expect double the lines to equal double the risk, but yellow lines do not behave in such an obvious and linear way. The risk is in fact greater, such that if you park on a double yellow line, the moment you are out of sight, a traffic warden and a CLAMPING VAN will appear to give you a ticket and clamp you.

Red lines – even if your car has diplomatic plates or no plates at all – i.e., it's the Queen's – parking on a red line means you're in big trouble. In fact the Queen was once towed away for parking on a red line – she'd pulled over to purchase a packet of JAMMY DODGERS and a copy of The Sun, and even though she'd left the hazards on they still towed her car away. The resultant £125 fine she had to pay to have her car released almost brought the monarchy to its knees. After seven appeals – the last of which was fronted by the Lord Chief Justice – the fine was rescinded and the monarch paid £730, 876 in damages – ALL PAID FROM THE PUBLIC PURSE.

The monarchy almost being brought to its knees.

Zigzag lines – in the world of parking this is the worst possible place you can leave your vehicle. Along with treason, it is the only offence in Britain still punishable by death.

Across the carriageway

Vomit – a rose-shaped smattering of dried puke on the pavement or road is almost certainly an indication that someone was EXTREMELY PISSED in that vicinity the previous evening. That said, it is permissible to park on it, though be warned, if it is particularly thick it might be obscuring a yellow or red line.

Police-horse poo – police horses outside football stadiums on match days will always DEFECATE in the road at the most inconvenient places. On average one out of every two football fans will step in it.

> SCORPIO CAR (bought between 24 October – 22 November)
> Don't be diverted from the road you're on. The B roads are much slower and you'll probably end up behind a tractor.

20. VEHICLE MARKINGS

Large goods vehicle rear markings

School bus -
only silhouetted
children allowed.

Work out the meaning of these yourself.

Hazard warning plates

When transporting anything that might blow up if someone 3 miles away strikes a match, you must display hazard information panels. The last thing you want if your vehicle does explode, KILLING FIFTEEN PEOPLE, is to be hit with a fine for not displaying the sign as well.

Pirates on board that haven't washed for so long they've become highly toxic.

Angry driver liable to spontaneously combust at any moment.

Highly dangerous radioactive substance aboard which is being taken somewhere to be dumped. It will then still be highly dangerous but not to the lorry driver who will be 300 miles away.

Large consignment of illegal immigrants aboard.

Vehicle containing vehicle containing hazardous material.

Other vehicle markings

 One of a series of markings that say nothing about the driver of the vehicle, but mark out the writer of the marking as a person who, rather mistakenly, thinks they are really funny. Other such markings include 'Terry is a wanker' and 'For a good time call 0209 9956776'.

 A marking enticing fellow drivers to call and comment on the driving prowess of the vehicle driver. No one in the history of the world has ever done so.

This marking indicates that your car has been keyed. If you catch the culprit the correct procedure is to take the key from them and flatten it by running it over in your car, thus carring their key.

ANNEXES

I. CHOOSING AND MAINTAINING YOUR BICYCLE

Make sure that:

- you choose a bike you like

- you have enough money to pay for it

- you own a sensible BELL and not one of those tinny child ones that wouldn't alert a shrew to your presence, let alone a massive great bloody car

- you don't need STABILISERS

- you are prepared for a lifetime of being called A TWAT.

You must:

- deeply RESENT all other road users

- remember your mother's birthday

> SAGITTARIUS CAR (bought between 23 November – 22 December)
> A great day for treating yourself to something new and socialising – so go out and get pistons.

II. MOTORCYCLE LICENCE REQUIREMENTS

There are many varied and complex rules regarding motorcycle licence requirements. If the following does not fully answer all your queries it is suggested that you pop along to your local Hell's Angel Advice Bureau. The heavily tattooed staff with poor hygiene standards are always on hand to offer friendly and helpful advice and, where NECESSARY, BEATINGS.

If you have a full car licence you can ride a bike up to 125cc as long as you pass a Compulsory Basic Training (CBT) course. If you don't pass the CBT you really shouldn't be driving a car.

If you have a full moped licence, well done, you can ride a moped.

If you have a partial TV licence you can watch people riding bikes up to 500cc, but only if you wear protective clothing.

If you have a dog licence you still need to take the CBT to ride a bike, but, if you pass, your dog can ride a tricycle.

You **MUST NOT** carry a pillion passenger if they would rather TAKE THE BUS.

III. MOTOR VEHICLE DOCUMENTATION

Driving is not simply a case of getting into a car and setting off, oh no, you need lots of bits of paper before you can even think about heading off – bits of paper that cost money.

Tax disc – sticking a note to your inside windscreen saying that your tax disc is wending its way to you through the post no longer cuts any ice these days. Your tax disc signifies that you have paid your road tax (even though only a tiny proportion of this money actually goes to maintaining and improving roads). At present there is no PEDESTRIAN TAX for using the pavements or indeed the roads. However, plans are afoot and if passed all pedestrians will have to display a disc in the top pocket of a shirt or as an arm patch at the ELBOW. Stepping outside your house without one of these discs will incur an immediate £50 fine that will increase by £1 per untaxed footstep you take.

Driving licence – in bygone days a driving licence was a raggedy SCRAP OF PAPER with barely decipherable writing on it. So if stopped by the police, you could produce a wax-crayon drawing done by a two-year-old and get away with it. Not so today. Nowadays you have to have a photocard licence. This represents another encroachment of the burgeoning STATE APPARATUS into our lives.

One of these MOT certificates is not genuine

MOT (Genuine) – every car has to pass an MOT test to ensure that it is roadworthy. If the car is in a decent condition it will get an MOT (Genuine). This fills the driver with a tinkle of satisfactionand smugness as they drive past smashed up cars that will never get an MOT (Genuine).

MOT (Dodgy) – once a car is too knackered to get an MOT (Genuine) it has to get an MOT (Dodgy). You can get these from mechanics (Dodgy).

Insurance – you need to be insured before you drive in case you smash into someone else's car. There is a dizzying array of different types of insurance available. When selecting which type to purchase, bear in mind the following principle. If you make a claim (even for a tiny amount, say £7.26) your premiums will quadruple overnight and you will be placed on a POOR CREDIT-RATING list – this means you will never be able to secure an unsecured loan or vice versa, ever again.

Vehicle registration document – yet another piece of paper you have to have before being allowed out on the roads. It's sometimes also (for unfathomable reasons) called the logbook. The totally brilliant thing about it is that it is absolutely free and you don't have to pass a test to get it. However, if you sell a car and forget to inform the authorities it will COST YOU A LOT OF MONEY, so perhaps it's not so brilliant after all. As with MOTs it is possible to get dodgy ones if you're intending to pull a bank job, though these are not free.

Production of documents – if a police officer asks you to produce your documents she or he means the above documents and not the title deeds to your house, your 100M SWIMMING CERTIFICATE or any other documents you might have in your possession. If you do not have them handy, you will be required to take them to a police station within seven days. If you are summoned to a police station, be prepared for the mother of all waits. You with your PATHETIC PILE of paper are totally inconsequential when, in the station, there are others that have committed heinous crimes. So take a novel (a crime one preferably) and bed down.

Losing and replacing documents

If you lose any of these crucial documents then you're about to waste a substantial proportion of your life. Getting replacement ones is very expensive, highly bureaucratic and a TOTAL PAIN. If you do send off for replacement documents and the replacement ones genuinely do get lost in the post – NO ONE ON GOD'S EARTH WILL BELIEVE YOU and it's time to scour the internet for a GOOD FORGER.

Documents in glove compartments

Glove compartments were originally designed for the storing of driving gloves until these UNNECESSARY and RIDICULOUS highway garments were outlawed in 1968. Today these receptacles are in truth more likely to contain all of the crap that mounts up on your travels - HALF-EATEN TWIXES, pencils, old parking tickets, 2p pieces, shopping lists, bills etc. DO NOT ever put any 'valuables' in your glove compartment. They will immediately vanish and be reincarnated as a BATTERED PACKET OF CRISPS.

IV. THE ROAD USER AND THE LAW

Road traffic law

The following abbreviated terms must be understood and memorised by every driver. A quick-fire test may be administered by police officers at the roadside or in the back of their vans. During these it is not necessary to wear handcuffs, but some of the more pernickety officers might insist. Go along with them, unless you want to end up sharing a cell with the hardest man in England who, due to his SEXUAL PERSUASION, will also insist on you wearing handcuffs.

Most of these legal provisions apply on all roads in Great Britain, but there are some exceptions. Incredibly, the definition of a 'road' in

England and Wales is different to the definition in Scotland. (HONESTLY, IT'S TRUE.) Therefore, if in Scotland, it might be worth checking that what you're driving along is in fact a road and not a 'wee cowering shimmering road beastie noo'.

Road Traffic Acts

Overtaking on hills, lanes and large animals Act 1970 OOHLALA

Dumping in Unauthorised New Garages Act 1954 DUNG

Pleasuring Innocent Motorway Personnel Act 1955 PIMP

Travelling Under Road Diversions Act 1987 TURD

Misuse of Improved New Green Engines Act 2002 MINGE

Carrying Onboard Carburettor Kit Act 1944 COCK

Chastising Useless Motorists Act 2004 CUM

Performing Unnecessary Braking Excellently Act 1980 PUBE

Bringing Up Meaningless Horseshit On Long Escapades Act 1977

BUMHOLE

Turning In Traffic Act 1998 TIT

Weaving Around Nearly Killing Enraged Roadusers Act 2000 WANKER

V. PENALTIES

Unlike in football, where a penalty is a good thing to get, when applied to driving, it is a bad thing. (Mad, isn't it?) There are a myriad of things for which you can be given penalty points ranging from 'Causing death to a hedgehog by dangerous driving' to 'Driving while naked save for a neck brace'.

Penalty points and disqualification

The system of penalty points was created to stop people driving badly. Occasionally they're awarded to stop people driving well, but this is always due to an 'administrative error'.

A driver who accumulates 12 or more penalty points within a three-year period (or 36 months, whichever is longer) will be banned from driving for a minimum of six months or for the longest number of months the declarer of the ban can count up to.

INTERESTING FACT

(Motorcyclists) The Queen owns the world's largest collection of vintage motorcycles, including a 1947 Norton which she used to ride to her coronation in 1953.

Penalty Table

OFFENCE	IMPRISONMENT	FINE	DISQUALIFICATION	PENALTY POINTS
Driving while under the influence of snuff	Unlikely, unless you continually sneeze during your trial	3 drachma	Half an hour	1–1.8
Causing death to a hedgehog by dangerous driving	Life	275 baht	Half an hour	302
Driving a juggernaut through a department store because you were peeling a satsuma	2 weeks community service	190 Canadian dollars	4 seconds	49,839
Driving naked save for a neck brace	Yes if male, no if female. (Reverse depending on sex/sexuality)	Completely and utterly	Whatever	-7
Driving really, annoyingly slowly	10–15 years maximum security	All your worldly possessions	3 months spread over 15 years	A number equal to, but not exceeding the number of stars in the known galaxy
Carrying a dead body in the boot	5–7 years, but we're all in a prison of our own making and have been given a lifetime sentence.	3 jars of honey	Until a week next Thursday	Pick a number, any number

New drivers

Telling a policeman that you've only recently passed your test will not wash if you overtake a speeding ambulance on the inside, maiming THREE OAPS in the process. Adding detail to the excuses like 'I just had to nip out and buy my gran some emergency LAVENDER WATER' will also not suffice.

While it is understood that the sheer elation of finally being legitimately allowed to drive can be considerable, particularly if it took you over fifteen attempts to pass your test, leniency is just not an option.

Other consequences of offending

If you don't get caught you will most probably be asked to be the driver on BIG BANK JOBS.

When you do get your licence back you have to drive around with an 'O'-plate on the back of your car. This alerts other drivers to the fact that you are an offensive driver so that they can STICK THEIR TONGUES OUT at you and pull funny faces and is akin to sixteenth-century stocks.

And worst of all, you might be forced to become a CYCLIST.

VI. VEHICLE MAINTENANCE, SAFETY AND SECURITY

Vehicle maintenance and safety

The golden rule of vehicle maintenance and safety is to make sure that everything is working. The other golden rule is to ensure that nothing is broken. If you stick to these two simple edicts you won't go far wrong and you'll enjoy your driving days to the full. Sadly, however, all too often people fall foul of these rules, which, in EXTREME CASES, can lead to your car not working.

Brake lights – at some point in the life of your car one of its brake lights will cease working. In the mind of the driver this is a relatively inconsequential thing. It does not need to be fixed straight away and need not entail taking the car off the road. In the mind of a police officer though this is a most heinous crime, right up there with the worst PREMEDITATED MURDERS. If spotted, a hastily assembled SWAT team will isolate your car, disarm you, whether you are armed or not, and then TAKE UP COVERING POSITIONS such that a specially trained police officer can safely approach the vehicle and say, 'Excuse me sir, did you know that one of your brake lights isn't working?' The correct response in this instance is, 'Oh no officer, I didn't, but I shall make haste to the nearest garage and have it seen to. Thank you for alerting me to it.' And then you drive off and forget all about it until the next time you're pulled over.

Windscreen washers – when your water supply is full there is much fun to be had turning them on in a densely pedestrianised area. When empty, filling it becomes one of those jobs that you keep MEANING TO DO but never quite get round to. Most drivers therefore only get their washers refilled when their car is MOT'd, meaning most cars only have their windscreen washers working at full capacity for about two weeks of the year.

Lights – your car is awash with lights: headlights, brake lights, fog lights, indicators, reverse lights, door lights and, in certain cases, small standard lamps fitted to the boot. The single, simple rule here is, don't leave them on. Well, do leave them on when driving at night or indicating or reversing etc., but don't leave them on when you're not actually driving the car. If you do you'll end up with a flat battery and have to enter into what is known as 'THE JUMP-LEAD SITUATION'. This involves having to do two things that most normal, decent folk hope never to have to do in their lifetimes. Firstly, you have to talk to a stranger and secondly, you have to attempt to sort out the problem yourself. Now, to people in the know, fitting jump leads and recharging the battery is the car equivalent of changing a plug. To the rest of us it's a MIND-BENDING CONUNDRUM that spells disaster whichever way you look at it. The best you can hope for is that the stranger you accost knows about cars and is kind-hearted enough to help without wanting to have SEX WITH YOU IN RETURN. Failing that dial 999 and alert all three emergency services.

Luggage – when taking your car on holiday it is imperative that you fill every single spare millimetre of your car's interior. The way to ensure you have followed this rule is to sit in the driver's seat and look in the rear view mirror; if you can still see out of the back, grab the third television set from the house (the one you'd decided not to take with you) and use it to plug the gap.

Warning displays – funny noises and strange lights on the dashboard. It is always best to ignore these occurrences. Only take notice of them once smoke starts BILLOWING OUT of the engine or the car is juddering so much any milk you have in it is turning to yogurt.

Tyres

Tread – you need lots of this on your tyres. If SPARKS ARE FLYING FROM YOUR WHEELS and you're cutting two deep grooves in to the road as you're driving, your tread is getting quite low and YOU'LL PROBABLY NEED NEW TYRES some time in the next year or two.

Flat – getting a flat tyre is another situation akin to getting a flat battery. Indeed that is why they both have the word 'flat' associated with them even though one is more literally correct than the other. It's meant to be easy to change a tyre; it's not. It involves tools, unscrewing, something called 'jacking', getting dirty and SCREWING. Even though in Formula 1 they do it in three seconds, the average person should set aside half a day at the very least to get the JOB DONE and, even if they do manage to fit a replacement tyre they'll have NO faith in it and will be convinced it will fall of at any second – most likely as you hit 70 mph on the motorway, which it probably will.

Pressure – tyres need air just like humans do. However, unlike the air humans' breathe, tyre AIR IS NOT FREE and will set you back in the region of twenty pence at most petrol stations. Alternatively, you can save the money by blowing the tyres up yourself, though this takes some puff and can take up to eight hours.

Vehicle security

There are a number of steps you can take to ensure the security of your vehicle:

• **Have a shit car** – on the whole the flasher the car is the more appealing it is to thieves. This is not entirely true, as the old adage 'some people will steal anything' proves, but if I was looking to nick a car, which I'm not, I'd rather take a brand SPANKING new motor than a clapped out old banger, unless it is really easy to do and then I might just steal it for a laugh, though just to reiterate, I wouldn't as I'm not a CAR THIEF.

• **Car alarms** – car alarms are utterly useless because they have never been known to go off when someone is actually trying to steal a car. They go off when someone is looking at a car, if a leaf falls on a car, if a BUTTERFLY FLAPS ITS WINGS IN NAMIBIA, in the middle of the night waking up an entire postal district or just because they feel like it. They will then stay on for three hours, stop for no apparent reason and then start up again sixteen seconds later.

- **Car keys** – after decades of research it is now generally accepted that leaving your keys in the ignition makes it easier for most thieves to steal your car.

- **Vandalism** – most vandals are simply bored TEENAGERS LOOKING FOR KICKS. To prevent them getting those kicks by smashing your car windows or running a key down the side of your car, either INTRODUCE THEM TO DRUGS or fund the building of a youth community centre several miles away from where you intend to park. Alternatively, you could vandalise your own car before they get the chance. Why should they have all the fun?

TV shows where they see how long it takes ex-cons to break into people's cars – these programmes (while highly enjoyable) actually show the uninitiated how to rob a vehicle and are responsible for the METEORIC RISE IN CAR THEFTS. The police would love to ban these shows but they enjoy them too much.

Servicing your car

It is generally recommended that you get your car serviced once a year, or if you are a car-lover, once every six months. People who leave five years between services are either SKINT or simply DON'T WANT TO FACE THE REALITY that they're driving a poor excuse for a car, that is on its last legs/wheels.

Washing your car

There are three ways to wash your vehicle:

Do it yourself – if you choose to wash your car yourself you can only do it on a Sunday morning. No one knows why, but on the occasions when another day has been tried, the very FABRIC OF SOCIETY begins to unfurl and civilisation as we know it starts to breakdown.

Take it to an automated garage car wash – there are usually four or five levels of wash to choose, from 'rubbish' to 'so clean the royal family could eat grouse off the bonnet'. The cost of these different types of washes varies considerably – however, the actual difference in cleanliness of your car is nil.

Visit a hand 'Valeting service' car wash – let's not beat around the bush here, these places are staffed by ILLEGAL IMMIGRANTS. However, no one is in the least bit interested in reporting them to the relevant authorities, as they tend to do a cracking job, especially on police cars.

CAPRICORN CAR (bought between 23 December – 19 January)
Lately life will have felt like being stuck in a slow moving traffic jam, which, seeing as you're a car, is probably pretty accurate.

VII. FIRST AID ON THE ROAD

In the event of an accident there are a few things you can do even if you have no training. (If, on the other hand, you have plenty of training – perhaps you are a doctor or a member of St John Ambulance – there are many things you can do, most of which we know nothing about because we're not trained.)

Panic – this involves virtually no training whatsoever and involves such actions as SCREAMING, HYPERVENTILATING, CRYING and in some cases, self-injuring.

Stand around and observe the carnage saying, 'OOH, THAT LOOKS NASTY' – this also involves little or no training beyond the ability to not panic in an accident situation and be able to say the words, 'OOH, THAT LOOKS NASTY.'

Call an ambulance – this can be achieved by dialling 999. However, due to staff shortages and traffic congestion you will then have to wait about an hour for the ambulance to actually arrive, so it might be worth purchasing a magazine to keep you occupied while you wait. Don't forget, of course, to ring your local radio phone-in show to complain about how long it took to arrive.

'Another sausage anyone?'

Deal with danger

Fire is one of the greatest dangers after a crash.
However, if having assessed the situation you are
confident that a further explosion is unlikely a
burning vehicle makes a handy barbecue.

Help those involved

DO talk about other people you know who have
been involved in accidents and are now fine, but
DO NOT talk about people who are now
PARALYSED FROM THE NECK DOWN and
can only communicate by winking.

DO NOT go into action-hero mode and
drag casualties from the vehicle if the accident
only involves someone's wing mirror being
dented lightly.

Provide emergency care

Follow the ABC of first aid.

A is for Alcohol – it can be quite traumatic to witness an accident, so make sure you know where the nearest pub is so that you can nip there and down a few swift ones if necessary.

B is for Breathing – if any of the casualties appear not to be breathing administer the kiss of life. As a general rule this does not usually involve using tongues and copping a feel at the same time.

C is for Comfort – gawping at the scene of an accident is far more pleasurable if you're relaxed and warm, so always have a foldaway chair and blanket in the car with you.

Be prepared

 Always carry a first aid kit.
This should include the following items:

- 1 crepe bandage
- 1 large pack of plasters
- 1 tube of antiseptic cream
- A pair of scissors
- A thermometer

However, when you come to open it you'll find it actually contains:

- 2 fags ends
- 1 plaster (USED)

VIII. DRIVING ABROAD

In the real Highway Code, you will find nothing about this most crucial aspect of driving. It is a TERRIBLE OMISSION and one we are proud to rectify within our humble guide.

Hiring a car

It is vital to accept that hiring a car once you have arrived in your selected destination, can add anything up to a week onto your trip – the paperwork alone can take four days. In the trade this is generally known as 'the-bloody-annoying-week-I-had-to-spend-trying-to-hire-a-car-and-for-some-reason-they-didn't-speak-English' syndrome. The best thing to do is add an extra week onto your holiday.

Foreign motorway service stations

Although extremely hard to get used to, motorway service stations in foreign countries actually serve food, not PLASTIC SHEETING dressed up as sandwiches. Eat as much as you can in these establishments, because sure as hell when you return to BLIGHTY and are reminded how crap and overpriced the food is in our service stations, you won't want to eat for months. They also stock large quantities of HARDCORE PORNOGRAPHY, including SPECIALIST TITLES, apparently.

The horn

Here in Britain a certain innate politeness means that one's horn is rarely, if ever, used. That doesn't apply abroad. In foreign climes, the nanosecond the lights change if you don't move instantly, a physical impossibility, everyone within a 15-mile radius will hoot their horn. Don't take it personally. They can't help it. Remain British at all times and simply doff your cap to your fellow motorists, before setting off at your leisure.

Dealing with foreign officials

Speeding while abroad and then claiming you simply got your miles and kilometres mixed up cuts absolutely no ice with foreign officials unless their maths is shit. The best thing to do is offer them a FISCAL BRIBE, in either sterling or dollars, or failing that take their entire extended family for a three-course meal (with beverages and petit-fours). This applies to any offence that you have committed, real or imaginary.

Twinning

It is a very common sight while driving abroad to see that some towns are 'twinned' with a counterpart town in the UK. We follow this practice in the UK and our messages tend to be polite, such as: 'Gorton twinned with the picturesque Spanish town, La Croza'. Abroad this gentle INTER-COUNTRY BONHOMIE is not pursued. So don't be shocked by signs stating things such as: 'Stuttgart twinned with Bicester – the dung-heap of Western Europe'. No offence is intended, but it is certainly taken.

Foreign guidebooks

If you haven't worked this out already every foreign guidebook entry is written by the son, daughter, niece or nephew of a hotelier/restaurant-owner/beerkeller/landlord. These books are quite simply dedicated to taking your trade into particular establishments. Ignore these bleatings. Instead find the most non-touristy off-the-beaten-track place and suffer hours of UTTER HUMILIATION, surrounded by groups of people who don't want you to be anywhere near them. (Note: Make sure that you inform the foreign guidebook about the place once you've been there so that it can be included in the next edition of the book, that way it will garner some much needed trade and won't remain off the beaten track for long.)

Foreign taxis

It is not uncommon for cabbies in foreign countries, to take little liberties with your lack of local knowledge. When these 'necessary diversions' result in your driver dipping in and out of surrounding countries, it is time to settle up.

The legal position

In certain countries, it is actually illegal to drive with even the slightest morsel of safety or responsibility. In these places a sort of free-for-all MENTALITY exists and it is best to treat the road as you would the British Grand Prix – burn some rubber, baby!

Asking for directions abroad

DON'T.